Joey Weisenberg's effect on how we participate in Jewish singing will forever impact on our relationship to Judaism and each other. While he has taken from the legacies of Goldfarb, Friedman and Carlebach, not to mention the hundreds of lesser known creators of nigunim, ultimately he is putting his personal stamp on our ever changing tradition and helping us all achieve transformation through music.
Elise Bernhardt
President and CEO
Foundation for Jewish Culture

More than any other art form music has urged a new creative vista for Jewish expression and practice in our era. By fusing theory, pedagogy, and deep knowledge and feel for music, Joey offers a precious map for those of us who believe that a community must be able to translate its sacred traditions and texts through art in order to know where it needs to go."
Stephen Hazan Arnoff, Executive Director of the 14th Street Y
Founder of LABA: The National Laboratory for New Jewish Culture

Joey Weisenberg is one of the greatest of the young Jewish musicians and teachers coming onto the scene today. He and his music are full of skill, sincerity, and passion. As a student of mine, he quickly learned the modulating modes and improvisational constructions of Cantorial music, and most importantly, how that music brings out the character of prayer. In Building Singing Communities, he thoughtfully presents innovations for the shul that reflect his experiences and experiments in the field of Jewish music. Joey's work will appeal to people from across the Jewish spectrum, and I eagerly await seeing what develops from these promising ideas.
Cantor Noach Schall
Author The Hazzanic Thesaurus and master teacher of Cantorial Music for over 60 years

To build and sustain Jewish community, Jews must find and lend their voices – every member of the mishpuchah must be given user-friendly tools to join in song... In Building Singing Communities, Joey Weisenberg, an unusually versatile musician and rousing facilitator, shares his experience and expertise in orchestrating Jewish communities in search of transcendence. The practical lyrics of this how-to guide help generate the deeply inspiring spiritual music that underlies the eternally singing collective of our people.
Rabbi Simkha Y. Weintraub, LCSW
Rabbinic Director, JBFCS National Center for Jewish Healing
Grateful member, Kane Street Synagogue, Brooklyn

Joey's unique vision for building inclusive, participatory singing communities is a much needed contribution to modern prayer groups, regardless of age, size, or affiliation. Having sung - and lead - in his High Holiday services for the past 3 years, I can attest both to Joey's innovations and insights in davenning experiences, as well as to his incredible talent and breadth of musical knowledge. Above all, Joey strives to build relationships through shared musical experiences, and with the practical tips and colorful analogies in this book, he makes it easy for you to embark on your own journey as a leader of prayer and song.

Aaron Bisman
Co-founder & President, JDUB

Joey Weisenberg has his finger on the pulse of today's "independent minyanim." In *Building Singing Communities* he shows us how to re-imagine the two core elements of your shul: building community and making music that enhances that community. There is so much here from which we can all learn. I highly recommend this book to professionals and laity alike.

Hazzan Henry Rosenblum
Forest Hills Jewish Center
Former dean of the H.L. Miller Cantorial School of the Jewish Theological Seminary

This book is more than an instruction manual: It is an expression of a philosophy—one in which musical quality truly matters, and to which we can all contribute. It is my hope that this book (like so many of Joey's classes at Mechon Hadar and elsewhere) will inspire Jews of diverse and varied backgrounds to take singing and davenning more seriously, and to recognize the power and beauty that they will unleash when they pool their musical energies—even as they direct their hearts towards their own unique and personal prayer.

Rabbi Elie Kaunfer
Co-Founder and Executive Director of Mechon Hadar

Building Singing Communities:

A Practical Guide to Unlocking the Power of Music in Jewish Prayer

BY

Joey Weisenberg

Foreword by Rabbi Elie Kaunfer

MECHON HADAR

A Publication of Mechon Hadar's Minyan Project

www.mechonhadar.org

CREDITS:
Illustrations: Julie Meslin
Editors: Sarah Schmerler, Nancy Ettenheim
Graphic Design: Ginny Prince

DEDICATION

For Lev Boaz and Moshe Ziv,
in memory of
Milton Boaz Ettenheim

TABLE OF CONTENTS

FOREWORD BY RABBI ELIE KAUNFER iii

INTRODUCTION v

Part I   Jewish Singing: The Communal Experience
CHAPTER 1 The Singing Core:
Musical Communication in Real Time 3
CHAPTER 2 The Architecture of Singing:
Setting up the Shul for Singing Together 9
CHAPTER 3 Building Momentum While Nurturing Beauty:
The Musical "Tipping Point" 13

Part II   Jewish Singing: The Individual Experience
CHAPTER 4 Gold's Four-Step Path to Melody Acquisition 19
CHAPTER 5 How to Sing a Melody 20 Times in a Row: Creating
Spontaneous Variations, Improvisations, and Interpretations 23
CHAPTER 6 Basic Jewish Music Theory 27

Part III   Teaching and Leading Jewish Music
CHAPTER 7 Teaching Melodies:
A Practical, Stand-Alone Class 37
CHAPTER 8 Leading Services:
For the Beginner Ba'al Tfilah 47
CHAPTER 9 The Artistry of the Ba'al Tfilah: Leading, Listening,
Responding, Creating 53

Part IV   Building Singing Communities
CHAPTER 10 Politics and Diplomacy...............................67
CHAPTER 11 Expanding the Musical Culture of the Community 73

Acknowledgements 77

Footnotes 79

Glossary of Yiddish and Hebrew terms 83

FOREWORD

I first learned from Joey Weisenberg at 4 a.m. in upstate New York. By 5 a.m., I realized I had met a ground-breaking Jewish music and prayer educator.

It was 2005, and Joey was leading a class at the annual Shavuot retreat for Kehilat Hadar, an independent minyan in New York known for its spirited traditional davenning. There is a long-standing tradition to stay up all night on Shavuot studying, ending with morning prayers at dawn. Joey had the toughest teaching slot of the night: the final hour. Since I knew Joey was a musician, I figured we would sing a bunch of songs, trying to keep our eyes open until sunrise.

But Joey announced at the beginning of the class: "We're going to learn one melody tonight." I did the math in my head: A 2-3 minute melody for an hour means singing it 20 times in a row! I wondered if there were some way I could sneak out the back without Joey noticing.

But I stuck around, and we sang that melody 20 times. It was the first time I ever *truly* learned a melody. That is: After the hour ended, I could teach that melody to someone else. I understood how it might work in davenning. I had a real sense of the rhythm and emotional high points.

Not only did we sing, but Joey had us move our bodies. During the hour, we clapped out the beat of the melody. Joey told us that Jews had lost their ability to connect to rhythm, and I knew I was Exhibit A. We stood up and danced our feet in time. Four beats, four stomps. Joey ended the class by drawing us closer, and, all standing, we sang the melody one last time. It was glorious.

Joey is at the forefront of a budding musical explosion in Jewish communal life. In the past decade, 90 grassroots, independent minyanim have sprung up in North America, most of them animated by a vision of participatory and engaged davenning. Some synagogues have started to explore other modes of prayer, departing from the 20th century model of rabbi and cantor on the bimah. The Klezmer Revival of the 1980's has trained and inspired a new generation of creative Jewish musicians, who breathe new life into old musical forms.

And yet, these advances still represent the cutting edge, not the typical Jewish musical experience. What would it take to take a world of "singing communities," as Joey calls them, to the mainstream? This book is the first step.

Joey is unusual because he feels at home in all the arenas where this musical revival is playing out. During the week, at Yeshivat Hadar, Joey runs melodies classes, like the one I experienced at 4 a.m., schooling a generation of young change agents in the art of Jewish singing. At the Kane Street Shul in Brooklyn, a 100 year old Conservative synagogue, Joey has spent the past four years working with the traditional synagogue framework, experimenting with new approaches to davenning and music. And as a mandolinist and guitarist, he has performed and recorded nationally and internationally with dozens of bands and ensembles, and shared his musical expertise in a wide variety of venues.

Joey's approach is appealing to a generation of Jews looking to take an active role in building their spiritual communities and connecting with each other and God through prayer. It encourages anyone to learn how to sing prayerfully, and offers practical tips for the more daring on how to teach melodies and lead congregations in prayer.

But this book – the first publication of Mechon Hadar's Minyan Project – is more than an instruction manual. It is an expression of a philosophy, one in which musical quality matters, and where we can all contribute to building communities around music. It is my hope that this book, like so many of Joey's classes, inspires Jews in multiple communities to take singing and davenning more seriously, and to recognize the power and beauty that can be unleashed when this is done.

– Rabbi Elie Kaunfer
Co-Founder and Executive Director of Mechon Hadar

INTRODUCTION

Az Yashir Moshe, U'v'nei yisrael, et ha'shira hazot...
"And so Moses sang, with all of the children of Israel..." - Exodus 15:1

In the last few decades, Jews around the U.S. and elsewhere have begun to re-explore their collective singing heritage – singing millenia-old *zmirot* (shabbat songs) around the Shabbat table, *nigunim* (wordless melodies) at *tisches* (tables) and gatherings, and rediscovering vast troves of Yiddish and Ladino songs, not to mention thousands of settings for *piyutim* (devotional poem-songs) from across the globe. By laying out practical strategies for creating music together, this book aims to re-activate our ancient musical heritage in ways that will empower us to find new beauty and spiritual awareness in our lives today.

Sometimes I wonder: if we've got a grand room full of musical treasures, and we've got the keys, why aren't we opening the door? We can make great communal Jewish music a reality all the time, not just a once-in-a-while occurrence. This musical potential is only unlocked, however, when we intentionally put the key into the lock and turn – and it's that easy! It happens when we take the time to study our musical past, when we have the confidence to come closer together, and when we commit to the ongoing process of re-learning how to listen to each other. Just think how far we could come if we treated the songs sung by our day-to-day lay synagogue community as seriously as we do the music created by professional stage musicians. We could create an atmosphere of both great beauty and drama in our spaces of prayer; we would value each and every individual in our community as a creative musician, and encourage his or her efforts in an attitude of musical collaboration. This reality is possible, if only we educate ourselves about (and hold ourselves to) aesthetic standards, if we raise the bar just a bit higher on what we can achieve together in beautiful, conscientious song.

People sing for widely divergent reasons – any one of which is meaningful enough, and probably reason enough, to consider the kind of community commitment I'm suggesting. Here are just a few:

- Music has always been intricately interwoven into Jewish life; when we sing today we feel connected with the great Jewish singers of centuries past – from King David to Yossele Rosenblatt.
- Singing allows us to communicate and express ourselves in ways that words cannot. An example is our yearning for the divine, or in the communication of our deepest sorrows or joys.
- Singing brings us closer to each other in a community, and teaches us how to listen to each other on many levels despite what may seem to be our vastly different back grounds and world-views.
- Singing marks time, and thereby puts us in touch with the rhythms of life; we see

how, throughout our liturgy, different types of melodies are used to differentiate between different times of the Jewish day, week, month, and year.

- Singing helps us to suspend our disbelief, like in the theater – to momentarily set aside our cynical world-views and stifling thought habits, and catch glimpses of the infinite wonder of the world.
- Singing is a platform for invention and creativity that allows us to improvise, create spontaneous harmonies and rhythms, and otherwise express our freedom.
- Singing is a healthy emotional carnival – a good channel for releasing all kinds of (pent up) emotions ranging from awe, fear, and contrition to overwhelming gratitude.

As I've visited more shuls around America, I've begun to notice that congregations of all sizes, locations, and denominations – from small *shtibls* (small shuls) to humongous, formal decorous Manhattan synagogues, from old established shuls to new-sprung independent *minyanim* (communal prayer quorums) – are all looking for ways to encourage singing in their congregations, both in shul and at home. They want everybody to get more involved in the singing as a collective, to make the large shul feel more *heimish* (home-like), to deepen their sense of community, and to create an atmosphere that feels *shabbosdik* (like Shabbat) and spiritual.

Within the walls of the synagogue, skilled singers have sung since the ancient days when the Levites sang in the *Beit Hamikdash* (ancient Holy Temple), *Chazzonim* (cantors), *ba'alei tfilah* (prayer leaders), and professional choirs have continued that tradition to the present day, creating varying interpretations of the liturgical texts that uplift the soul. Singing by the whole community during davenning, however, is a more modern innovation. First begun in chasidic *shtibls* several centuries ago, it slowly expanded into mainstream Jewish shuls in the last one hundred years – especially as various streams of Jewish observance and music began to merge in America. Close to a century ago, for example, Rabbi/Cantor Israel Goldfarb of the Kane Street Synagogue in Brooklyn began publishing books of music that were designed to be sung by the entire community. True, some have felt that communal singing has always been a distraction from the true davenning experience of old, and have gone so far as to say that communal singing has led to the "cheapening, trivialization, and vulgarization of the sanctity and dignity of synagogue worship." [1] Be that as it may, however, in recent years, thousands of Jews (including myself) have begun to reconnect with the davenning experience *because of the beauty and energy of the song that accompanies it;* we've taken part in a surge in Jewish spirituality and musical creativity of a kind that only song, sung in community, could convey. I'm more than willing to listen to "music's" detractors; but I also feel firm in my convictions, born of personal experience: communal singing is here to stay. Our task now is to make it as beautiful and aesthetically sensitive as possible, and to create a situation in which that singing graciously complements the Divine conversation of davenning.

This book is a practical "how-to" musical manifesto for Jews who want to foster the development of more singing around them, both in the shul and around the table. For community leaders who have an intuitive sense of the need to create a more engaged singing community, this book provides some specific language to describe it to their congregations. For musicians who have a lot of musical skill but don't know how to use it in a shul or at a *tisch*, this book provides some basic Jewish musical background, offering tools for how you can become an active contributor and teacher of Jewish music in your community. For cantors, *ba'alei tfilah,* and *shlichei tzibur* (community prayer leaders) who know the liturgy, *nusach* (solo cantorial chant), and many melodies – this book may help you to pilot "spontaneous Jewish choirs" that support your singing by actively listening and responding in real time. Most importantly, this is for all those who want to sing and create lovely ongoing musical moments with others.

On a final note, this book is not necessarily meant to be read in its entirety. If you would like to focus exclusively on one or two sections of this book – and ignore others – that's just fine. Skim Chapter Seven, for instance, and just learn how to lead a class; or prepare yourself mentally for leading an upcoming service, say, in Chapter Nine. It's just my hope that, ultimately, this collection of strategies will come to your aid; that with it, you'll re-actualize the talents and potential of your community, reaping the benefits of re-starting what is, in fact, our beautiful, longstanding tradition of collective Jewish song.

For easy reference, I have included a glossary of Hebrew and Yiddish words used in this book. See pages 83 and 84.

Part I

Jewish Singing: The Communal Experience

Kane Street Nign

Traditional, adapted by Joey Weisenberg
from M. Beregovsky's collection

Sometimes a singer cannot reach the higher notes. Another man comes to his aid and sings in a loud tone. This gives to the first man, also, the ability to raise his voice. It is a result of the communion of two spirits, wherein each becomes a partner in the other's strength. [2]

– The Koretzer

Music changes when other people enter the scene, often miraculously and for the better. The same note I was playing on the guitar by myself an hour ago sounds drastically different when it combines with a drummer's beats. The note I'm singing might sound like a different note altogether when somebody sings an unexpected harmony. Or, that note I played might gain a brand new energy when I know somebody else is listening or whispering "bravo"! Theoreticians describe the interactions of musical overtones, but mostly what I feel is the interactions of energies. Often these energies add up to much more than the sum of their parts. What's more, they create a combined, unpredictable magic that can only be experienced once, for next time it will change. Shared music, in short, is ephemeral, a product of the here and now.

The good news is that this experience need not be limited to performing musicians; it's magic is open to anybody who'll take the time to sing a *nign* (wordless melody) with a friend or community, or simply to listen closely while somebody else sings. When we hear words like "community," "collective," and "cooperative," we imagine coming together to support each other in creating realities that exceed our own abilities and imaginations – and rightly so. This section will offer practical advice for how to gather people together to sing in a communal way in the best sense of the word, where we make best use of all the different energies that people bring to the table, allowing people to create a truly collective musical magic.

To be sure, there are ways that the private magic of music can disappear when others enter the scene. The beauty of that note that sounded so full, so spiritual while rehearsing, may suddenly disappear when others are watching. The teacher intimidates the student and suddenly the student can't seem to remember anything he seemed to know so well at home. The singing is out of tune. And finally, a less-than-receptive audience may simply not understand the music, and summarily dismiss it. Since collective ventures can go either way – for the better or the worse – we have to develop better **strategies** for tipping the balance in favor of a beauty that is totally focused, rather than scattered, that can truly foster communal, in-the-moment inspiration. The concepts in this section – creating a singing core, standing in the center of a small room, paying close attention to the details of other people's singing – all aim to foster **focus**. They may sound simple, yet they effectively remove many of the common roadblocks that arise in communal situations, paving the way for creating a shared space in which divine inspiration can potentially enter.

The Singing Core: 1
Musical Communication in Real Time

Think about it, the most common-sense strategy for developing the kind of "singing together" I'm talking about is for singers to get physically closer. Hence, every congregation that aims to take its singing energy to the next level must develop a core group of singers who stand close together, directly surrounding the *ba'al tfilah* (prayer leader). I like to call this group the "Spontaneous Jewish Choir" and its participants "musical *gabbaim* (prayer assistants)," but this singing core is not a new idea at all. In many ways, it's actually a return to a centuries-old shul setup where, for generations, the *meshoririm* (choristers) gathered around the *chazzan* (cantor) at a low-level *bimah* (platform) in the center of the room to sing spontaneous harmonies.

Musical Communication in "Real Time"

When we stand close together, we are able feel immediate connections with other singers, to clearly hear and respond to each other's voices in **real time**. What this means is that we're not only looking for people to sing at the same time as each other, but to actually *sing together in ways that allow them to respond* to each other's musical subtleties. I've stood in the balcony at countless large synagogues and noticed people singing four different parts of the same melody at the

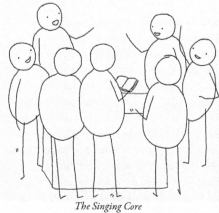

The Singing Core

same time, completely oblivious to the fact that the people in the other corners were wrapped up in singing totally different sections of the melody. When people are loosely spaced around a room, they may all be singing at the same time in a literal sense, but they're not necessarily singing *together* – in any emotional, or dare I say it, aesthetic, sense of the term. Who can blame them? Often they can't even tell if they're singing the same passage together or not; they're just too far away to hear.

What this means is that a formal piece of music, or a simple sing-song prayer, or a wordless nign – or whatever – doesn't reach its full potential when the people vocalizing can't hear each other's musical subtleties.

To be sure, I've often found myself in non-optimal music situations, and survived them, and even had lots of fun. I've led klezmer bands stretched out across city blocks while parading through the noisy Lower East Side of Manhattan, and a marching band spaced out a hundred feet between each musician while marching 500 Jews between the dinosaurs at the museum of Natural History. But while these situations are sometimes fun for their very novelty or because they are themselves walking parties, they don't truly facilitate musical connection. A klezmer band gets people dancing when it's grooving close together, focused on a dance floor. A marching band rouses the crowd with a powerful wall of sound when its members are marching close together or, conversely, sitting side by side in the bleachers, rather than spaced out across the football field for dazzling visual effect.

One of my favorite teachers, Rabbi Simkha Weintraub, jokingly relates the story of how, after a few private Pilates lessons, the teacher informed him that she had "never seen a person whose head is so detached from his body." Pilates, you may know, is the physical practice that suggests that all movement should emanate from the central core of one's body, and

thereby create unified motion and build strength. Similarly, in a shul, singing must emanate from a central core of singers, who strengthen the overall singing effort. Singers sound better when they are close to the core, just as arms need the support and connection of the torso in order to function. What's more, singing that emanates from a core also creates an atmosphere in the room – for those who aren't yet singing – that wouldn't occur if the musical energy were spread out, pell-mell.

Arms function better when connected to the torso

False Premise: Spacing out the Singers

Many well-intentioned people think that you must disperse the good singers throughout the room, so that the singing "reaches more people." Hence, they'll assign Harry to sit in one corner and Morty in another, while Simcha is marooned, somewhere in the bleachers, bringing up the rear. The problem is that when people sit far apart, they can't follow along with either the leader or each other, and eventually stop singing. They've lost the immediate connection with the other singers, and at best end up with a situation in which they are, indeed, singing at the same time, but not truly *together.*

Spacing out the singers

Here's another illustration of what I'm talking about: What happens when you separate the logs of a fire? The wind easily blows them out. But when you bring the same logs close together and light the match, you can get a raging bonfire. Spread out the singers throughout a huge sanctuary and what's likely to happen? The singing energy will die down. But bring people close together in the center, and you'll ignite a "singing bonfire" – even in a large space.

Centralized Singing Leads to Centralized Leading

The Singing Core also creates an incredible powerhouse that you, as *ba'al-tfilah*, can use to amplify your voice, and, by extension, your musical intentions. When you lead a congregation in prayer, you are steering the congregation, like a large car. The musical *gabbaim* (assistants) that stand around you become your "power-steering" mechanism. Rather than having to yank a wheel around a hundred times, drivers often take advantage of power steering, so that they can turn the car with only a slight nudge of the wheel. Similarly we want a slight "nudge" in our singing to create great change in the timbre of the room. In the same way that engineers configure a car's gears to do this, we must configure our singers around us and teach the responsiveness and listening that allows "musical power-steering."

Musical *Gabbaim* (Assistants) – Spontaneous *Meshoririm* (Choristers)

At the beginning of every service, I invite anybody and everybody to surround me or the other *ba'al tfilah* saying, "Please come join me here at the *shtender* (lectern) to sing harmonies, *whether you know what you're doing or not.*" You'll have to say this at the beginning of every service, for as many months and years as it takes for people to get the idea. Of course, ahead of time I've already drafted a few people to stand with me to make sure it works. I ask for at least six people, but it's fine if the entire shul wants to stand in the middle with you! Each of these musical *gabbaim* are responsible not just for singing, but for paying close attention to the cues and direction of the *ba'al tfilah*.

Inviting anybody to sing, of course, brings its own risks and rewards. Of course, from my (somewhat selfish) point of view as musical leader, I hope that more than a few musically knowledgeable, in-tune, rhythmically inclined singers accept the invitation. It sometimes happens that way. But equally often, you'll get a mixed group of talent which will routinely include:

- The Tone-Deaf – and LOUD! – Guy (there's always one)
- The Soprano Soloist who has not had enough stage time in recent years
- The Singer-Who's-Not-Paying-Attention
- The person who insists on singing all the syllables with different accents from you, to prove how Hebraically correct he is
- The out-of-time *shtender* pounder; the over-enthusiastic, loud pounder
- The old guy who sings three beats behind the group as a form of attention-seeking behavior

Now, however, let's not forget: The main purpose of gathering this rag-tag (though sometimes amazing!) group of singers is to create communal musical energy – *not to create musical perfection*. So, of course, everybody is invited to participate. Our prayer service isn't a performance, it's a community effort, to which everybody contributes in his or her own way. It's certainly helpful (and essential) to have people who know what they're doing; but it can be helpful in unpredictable ways even if they don't. As the teaching goes, the TZiBuR (public) is made up of: *Tzadikim* (Righteous), *Beinonim* (In-betweeners), *Rashaim* (Wicked). This inclusive vision of community applies to the musical skills of a singing public as well, and we can't deny people their place in the musical mix.

Abandoning Perfection – But Attaining Art

That's right, getting close together is no guarantee of good singing. Consider for a moment the point in the service on festivals and the High-Holy Days when the *kohanim* go up as a group for their blessings and respond to the chazzan's "Y'varech'cha..." with their own miraculously atonal variations. Or, I like to think of the way my grandfather, may his memory be a blessing, would wait until we had all gotten three words into Shabbat kiddush, and then proceed to start conspicuously from the beginning so that the whole thing was always off kilter (and that's when we were sitting close around the table)! In short, at least when you're close together, you have some chance at singing together, even if it doesn't end up always working out.

Professionalism isn't what we're after. We want an informal mob. An oozing cultural comfort that'll prove a soft nest for nurturing good song. Being informal, however, doesn't mean abandoning the quest for improvement; actually, behind this informality you'll find yourself constantly needing to guide individuals towards participating in ways more helpful to the group-song success of the whole. For the Tone Deaf – but LOUD! – Guy, or equally the Soprano Soloist, you might praise the beauty of their voices, but suggest that in a "choir situation," such as this, their voices could best be used if they tried "blending a little more with the surrounding voices"(translation: they ought to sing more softly). You may ask the Too-Loud-*Shtender*-Pounder to pound a bit later on, so that we can "build momentum" now. And as for the tone-deaf, but utterly nice fellow who just doesn't "get" my instructions, period, there are times when I've changed the entire key of a song or series of melodies to match the monotone that he felt comfortable singing. Sometimes, there's nothing you can do, and you must just laugh to yourself and think: Maybe that person is none other than Eliyahu Hanavi (Elijah the Prophet) – and who am I to say?!

Often, however, the results are far more promising, with potentially amazing amateur results: great energy, communal connections, and lots of active, respectful listening. I can honestly say that some of my proudest musical moments have come in the company of amateur singers who are pouring their hearts out in communal song.

Fostering Followership – How Leaders Grow from the *Amud* Up

The Singing Core, or the Spontaneous Jewish Choir that we create every time we daven, is all about cultivating a musical "**followership**" in the shul. As much as a leader needs to lead, followers need to follow. The leader lights the match, but the followers grab hold of what's happening at any moment and take it to a higher level. "Followership" and "Leadership" are not rigidly defined, as leaders one week may become followers the next week. It's an ever-shifting model of paying attention to each other, in which everybody takes charge and follows at different times, depending upon the needs of the situation.

As an added benefit, as this process of direct communal engagement unfolds over time, the *amud* (Torah table) and its singing Core becomes a **training ground for new leaders**. Eventually, the leader can step aside, and behold: there are seven other competent leadership-ready responders who are already comfortable being up there. What's more, when a professional *chazzan* (cantor) or a really fabulous *ba'al tfilah* (prayer leader) is leading, he or she happily finds a supportive core of involved daveners creating an active and connected room – the way it used to be for *chazzonim* in the old world where people were deeply attached to the *chazzan's* chanting.

However, be prepared: when this process of nurturing a singing-core of *gabbaim* first gets started, somebody will inevitably raise the objection, "Doesn't the core make others (who are not in the core) feel left out?" To be sure, there are some people who are not going to join a central unit of singers standing up so visibly before the kahal for a whole host of reasons: because they want to stay in their *makom* (place), or because they don't feel confident enough, or because they prefer some space and privacy in their prayer. These are important considerations. Amongst those who don't join the core, there will be a few who resent the singing because they don't like it, and a few who feel "left out," and a few grumpy old-timers who resent the intrusion of new energy into a place they consider to be their domain, and maybe one woman with perfect pitch who cannot stand the out-of-tune singing...BUT... So many others will be glad that something beautiful and engaging is happening in the room, even if they are not in the center of it, and some will gradually learn that they can become a part of it themselves, which will then make it even more beautiful. Undoubtedly, you'll find you'll have to weigh some very noteworthy pros and cons; mostly however, things boil down to effecting a delicate balance between the feelings of a few people who feel "left out of the singing" (because they choose to sit on the perimeter), against not having any unified singing at all; and in the latter situation it's my opinion that everybody loses out. Why forfeit the benefits of communal singing to entropy, or territorialism, waiting for a consensus that may never arrive?

The Architecture of Singing: 2
Setting up the Shul for Singing Together

Leading from the Center of the Room

A *ba'al tfilah* must lead from the center to be closer to the people he is leading. That way, the maximum number of people can follow in the immediate (not post-facto) way we've described.

Locating in the center of the room fosters a sense of "talking with" rather than "talking at" and creates, on the very simplest level, the shortest distance between two points – the "leader" and "the led." Moreover, leading from the center of the room is no innovation – in fact, it's the place from which Jews lead davenning for most of the past two thousand years. [3]

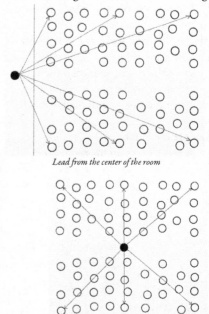

Lead from the center of the room

"Goodbye, *Bimah*"

In most shuls around the country, the main architectural impediment to real-time musical communication is the looming *bimah* at the front of the room. A tall frontally oriented *bimah* immediately detaches a leader from his singers and from his congregation. This eliminates any chance at "musical power-steering" that we discussed earlier. So here's one major and basic rule of creating Singing communities: **Ditch the *Bimah*.**

Bimot (plural, bimah) in the front of the shul emerged only in the last century or so and it's my considered opinion that they encourage a frontal, performance-oriented and ultimately passive mentality that leaves a *ba'al tfilah* feeling exposed and lonely and undercuts ongoing attempts at communal engagement in song. I've never seen a shul with a frontal *bimah* that really made full use of the talents and cooperation of its congregants. To be sure, the *bimah* makes for a nice *visual* experience, but an awful *aural* one. Think of it like you would a classic, proscenium stage, and you'll realize that, as in a Broadway show, the rabbi and cantor seem, to the "audience," to magically appear from their dressing rooms backstage all prepared to put on their stage-show, which is raised up above for all to see. But this does not help when people want to be a part of the show – or even at very least to engage with the *chazzan* in the centuries-old give-and-take of traditional davenning.

Not long ago I was co-leading a workshop at the Cantors Assembly Annual Convention, which took place in the huge sanctuary at the beautiful Park Avenue synagogue. I was talking about this very issue and I started deliberately walking down from the *bimah* and into the middle of the room to make my point– you know, the one about how important it is to be close to the rest of the congregation in order to hear them? Suddenly, up above in the gallery, the video cameraman began frantically waving at me, telling me to stop. Apparently, I had left the perfectly crafted rectangle of his video frame. He was concerned about the visual picture; I was concerned with the auditory one.

Being in the center "ups the game" of the leaders. A teacher, for example, who teaches from the middle of the room is forced to be more dynamic, to turn around to reach people and make eye contact, to work the room a bit. The same goes for a *ba'al tfilah* who leads from the center of the room: suddenly, the prayer-leader and the congregation awake into a much more direct communication with each other – and we hope, by extension – with the Divine.

Remove the Pews

In order to set up the room for ideal communal singing, you might have to change the seats in order to get the *amud* in the middle. If there are fixed pews in your shul, you can

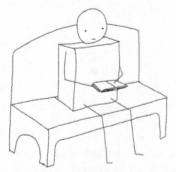

expect a ten-to 20-year battle to remove a section (or ideally all) of the pews so that a *shtender/amud* can be put in the middle, surrounded by flexible, movable seats. Simply put, when you sit in a pew, you tend to become a pew. Pews prevent movement, and thereby prevent comfortable singing.

Have you ever heard this refrain, "We can't take the pews out – they just went *in* seven years ago!"? Perhaps books like this will spare a few future shul remodelings from including pews or fixed, frontally oriented seat-

ing in the first place. If you already have pews, and you cannot immediately remove them, then don't delay – just forge ahead and move the davenning to the center of the room and let the physical architecture catch up later.

No Sound Systems!

Sound systems work against real-time musical communication. True, they do let people *hear* the leader, but what they are hearing is a "latent sound"; namely, by the time they hear the singing, it's already happened, and the congregation can't respond in real time. Imagine trying to sing together with someone through an online video camera, or on the phone: While a sound system in a big room may provide a quicker connection than a distant phone connection, it still lets people engage only after the fact, which means that the communication will be at best slightly detached from real-time.

We must be able to pick up directly on the singing going on around us, feeling the vibes directly from the leader, feeling the tones merging together, as a SPONTANEOUS JEWISH CHOIR. We, as human beings need to assume the role of sound-system, as a singing Core. Too often, the reality is that an (electric) sound system encourages people to sit further apart from each other, to spread out around the room, because they figure they can "hear" from any spot in the room. Just as quickly, they forget their role as active, rather than passive, singers, and lose touch with just how necessary we feel they are to ensuring a beautiful, cohesive whole.

That goes for the shul leadership, too. A rabbi and cantor must be willing to (and be encouraged to) sit with everybody else, so that people can interact with and hear their voices directly with no sound reinforcement.

Humans become the sound system

Relocate to the Smallest Possible Room

There is a convenient solution to many of these architectural problems inherent in large sanctuaries: Downsize! My

Small room brings people together

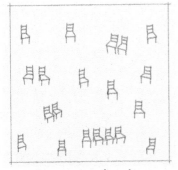

Large room spreads people apart

rule of thumb has always been, find the smallest possible room that accommodates the number of people you expect. A small room inherently creates a singing core, makes it easier to leave the *bimah* (because it's not built into the room), and removes the perceived need for a sound system (chances are, there won't even be a sound system in it to use!).

A small room that is full, even though "full" in such a space may amount to a scant 20 people, is going to feel much more exciting than a big room that can accommodate 400, but in which only 200 show up (yes, that's ten-times more!). So pack them in. Several feet closer makes a big difference. Imagine you're throwing a dinner party – it'll always seem more successful, the conversation livelier, when every table is full of happy, chattering people and the room is abuzz with their noise. A small room multiplies whatever energy is put into it; a big room lets it seep out and dissipate. So don't pick a big room if you can help it unless you know you've got enough attendees to fill it to capacity.

Won't people be disappointed? Our chapel/community space isn't much to look at...

Oftentimes smaller rooms are less ornately decorated, so they have less visual appeal. But plain has its advantages. Fewer distractions and a humble vibe in the air are qualities that lend themselves to increased singing focus and sincere davenning. As for sound quality, small rooms, literally, rock: the absence of fancy, upholstered chairs and wall-to-wall carpeting as well as a focused sound environment makes the room much more acoustically alive. In my book, grassroots wins out over grandeur...

Upholstery Go Home

Carpets, pillowed chairs, hanging tapestries, and other cloth materials capture sound and trap it. One reason that old urban synagogues (even large ones) have proven so much more resonant than newer ones (i.e., most suburban shuls from the 1950's) is that their interiors often featured hardwood floors and simple, uncushioned seating. True, the seats were less comfortable, but then again, people came to shul to daven, not to settle into a seat. Old, traditional shuls, by and large, had a much more "live" feeling to them – with people milling around, plenty of extraneous noises, but also a deeply resonant sound when the choir and *chazzan* began to sing. Today we can emulate the acoustics of days past by removing some of the sound-trapping extras in our decor and getting back to basics.

To summarize: In order to encourage real-time musical communication, create a core of singers that leads from the center of a simple, small room!

Building Momentum while Nurturing Beauty: The Musical "Tipping Point" 3

By now, we've explored the importance of establishing a Singing Core and setting up a room for optimized singing. Later on we'll explore the stylistic elements of Jewish music. But first, here are a few more key factors that help a community develop its musical momentum. These are the final touches that guide a community past what I call the *musical tipping*

point – a kind of temporal and psychological threshold over which a room full of bodies and voices transforms into a greater-than-its-parts gathering of additive, spontaneous energy.

Imagine pushing a heavy boulder up a hill. Before the crest of the hill, each and every step requires an enormous amount of effort and expended energy. After the summit, the boulder is going down the hill on its own accord, and you're riding the energy downhill. This process works the same way when

Musical tipping point

you're trying to get a room of people to sing together. At first, it feels like slow going, and nobody seems to be helping you. But if you're lucky, you may reach the tipping point of the musical room, and then the singing ball will start to roll on its own, generating its own musical momentum-with just a little bit of creative steering.

Body Language and Movement

Subtle movements and positive postures can have an enormous effect on the energy of the room. Each person is responsible for composing himself or herself in a way that suggests

positive engagement. One moping, bored-looking person can sap the energy of the room. By contrast, a joyous smile, a sway to the music, or a prayerful *shuckle* (rocking) can disproportionately enhance the energy of the room!

Creating a positive body language is difficult for many American Jews, as Jews have shed much of their movement traditions in the last century in an effort to "look normal" and assimilate. Other ethnic groups have no such problems. One time I was playing a concert of Yiddish music at a nursing home for a crowd that was largely composed of old Jewish and Hispanic folks. We started a

blaaaaah....

(Jewish) *freylakhs* (fast dance rhythm), and all the elderly Hispanic women immediately started clapping, smiling, moving, and some of them even pulled themselves up on their canes and began dancing excitedly. The elderly Jewish women, by contrast, remained almost entirely unchanged in countenance, as if the change to the faster dance music had never occurred. I was struck by the fact that this was their traditional music – and they had no idea what to do with it!

That said, our tradition is packed with movement, just as it is with music. The reason that "Tof" (drum) and "Machol" (dancing) are mentioned right next to each other when

describing Miriam's dance at the Red Sea is that in older times, to have drumming without dancing was unthinkable. They were two sides of the same coin. These days, however, when we do get around to dancing, it's usually with a big show of doing so at weddings and bar-mizvah events and other exclusively simcha-oriented moments, which may be why people are so intimidated by trying. Take a cue from some of the older folks who remember how to dance Jewish – and notice their small, humble movements!

Subtle dancing is okay!

Think about it: Prayer is traditionally accompanied by *shuckling* –a gentle rhythmic swaying that keeps the blood and spirit flowing. (*Shuckling*, we are told, resembles the trembling that the entire Jewish people did in God's presence at Mount Sinai.) If your body is stiff, so will your prayer be. By contrast, just a little bit of swaying greatly adds to a loose feeling in the room, and greatly enhances the music. *Shuckling* is an in-and-out motion that mimics the breath; it helps us to "breathe our prayers," which brings them to life.

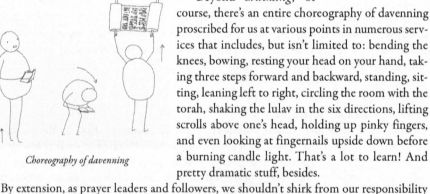

Shuckling

Beyond *shuckling*, of course, there's an entire choreography of davenning proscribed for us at various points in numerous services that includes, but isn't limited to: bending the knees, bowing, resting your head on your hand, taking three steps forward and backward, standing, sitting, leaning left to right, circling the room with the torah, shaking the lulav in the six directions, lifting scrolls above one's head, holding up pinky fingers, and even looking at fingernails upside down before a burning candle light. That's a lot to learn! And pretty dramatic stuff, besides.

Choreography of davenning

By extension, as prayer leaders and followers, we shouldn't shirk from our responsibility to assess how we are carrying ourselves at all times. How proud or humble do we look at any given moment? Indeed, we should stand humbly before the Almighty, like it says above the holy arks in many shuls, *"Da Lifnei Mi Atah Omed"* (Know before whom you stand); yet we should also seek to walk with pride, as we say in *Shacharit* (morning services) , *"V'tolicheinu 'kom'miyut' l'artzenu...* (to walk upright...to our land)." Conscientious purveyors of Jewish prayer are always trying to effect some kind of balance: an inner compromise, if you will, between shame and arrogance. Telegraphing pur-

Humble or proud...or a balance of both

posefulness to others has its merits. So no matter what, always try to take some pride in what you're doing – and infuse it with a little bit of playful joy.

Using the Details: Extra-Melodic Responsa and Intentional Silence

Communal responses and accompaniments are another important factor in effecting the musical tipping point in any singing service. Far from being expendable bits of marginalia, these traditional moments of give-and-take between *kahal* (congregation) and *ba'al tfilah* have proved liturgically inspiring and aesthetically effective for many generations. And I think they're indispensable. When you, as *ba'al tfilah*, hear a congregation reciting a hearty "AMEN," you are reinvigorated in your davenning, feeling that you have the necessary support, and that you're not davenning in a vacuum. Your reinforced energy, in turn, re-inspires the *kahal*. But these communal responses are not limited to "Amen." Any community should train (or retrain) its congregants to participate in the following ways:

- Saying *"Amen"*, and *"Baruch Hu U'varuch Sh'mo"*, in all the appropriate places. A good leader will clearly cue the *kahal* with a short break after the opening section of the *bracha* (blessing).
- Singing harmonic chords underneath the *chazzan's* improvised *nusach* (chant). Singing short, communal-response *nigns* (wordless melodies). These are actually part of the *nusach*, and are found in abundance on the high holidays. For example, in the High Holiday Musaf, the *chazzan* gets a five-second break while the congregation asserts the following phrase

Communal refrain Misod Chachamim

- Improvising musical responses between phrases of a melody: Much like a trombone does in a Dixieland band, a good singer or two can make up intermittent "nai nai nai" responses or contrapuntal bass lines at the end of melodic phrases that give continuity to a piece of music. This helps everybody know that the melody is not over, but rather, that it's just a long note, waiting for the next one to start.
- Mumbling the continuous undertone of davenning. This kind of low-level, bumble bee- like sound maintains a feeling of aesthetic motion, and keeps an energy in the room when nothing overtly musical is happening.
- Crafting and fostering *Intentional Silence* during those free moments of the davenning that are without *nusach* or song.

The Beauty of Intentional Silence: it's why we sing!

That last point was critical, and I want to emphasize it here. A serious singing community knows how to be quiet when the time is right. Silence is the aesthetic opposite of sound; silence creates the crucial balance to singing, a necessary foil, without which, all our sonic efforts would be in vain.

Good prayer leaders and song-ful *gabbaim* are vigilant to allow ample time for quiet in any given service structure. For example, when the hubbub of the pre-*Amidah* (central prayer) half-kaddish is coming to a close, when the shuffling sounds of our feet die down and the silent Amidah starts, there should descend upon the room a noticeable quietude – a freedom from any distracting sound. This is the main period of silence in our service, the opportunity to take a breath, turn inward, and give over to prayer. Similarly, there is the practice of being silent for a noticeable moment before saying *Sh'ma Yisroel* ("Listen, o Israel"). Our liturgical service has many aesthetic ups and downs built in. Sometimes we're supposed to be loud and joyous. Other times still. We're tying to draw out the beauty in each of them, to deepen the extremes.

My teacher, Cantor Noach Schall routinely shows me long compositions that he's painstakingly composed. He almost always half-jokingly points to the composition and declares, "The best part of this composition is..." and points to the big long rest, where no music is happening - where the silence breaks through.

Silence ought to remind us that a "singing community" is really a "listening community." While a singing community may produce beautiful harmonious melodies on a

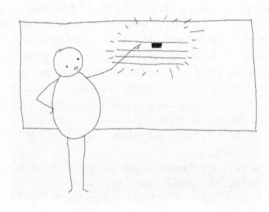

The best part of this composition is the...........silence

regular basis, have rhythmic intensity, and foster an exciting and contagious environment, the most important element of a functioning singing community is that people are continually developing their abilities to listen to each other and engage with each other – in other words, to PAY ATTENTION. Singing is not just a process of making noise through your throat and mouth-it is also a process of listening to what others are producing, and working together to create a larger beauty. We aim to pay attention to each other, to the prayer, and to the moment we're in, so that singing and the life surrounding it remain fresh and we avoid the pitfalls of habitual rote process.

PART II:

JEWISH SINGING: THE INDIVIDUAL EXPERIENCE

Laba Nign

Joey Weisenberg

Hadar Nign

Joey Weisenberg

Relaxed 3,3,2

Shalom Aleichem

Joey Weisenberg

Slow, pulsing

Sha-lom a - lei-chem mal'-chei ha- sha - reit   mal - a - chei___   el - yon

mi___   me-lech mal-chei ham-la - chim   ha - ka - dosh   ba-ruch hu

Gold's Four-Step Path to Melody Acquisition 4

The basis of any singing community is the individual's encounter and developing relationship with the melody. A friend of mine who loves to sing, [4] describes what he calls the "four-step path to melody acquisition," which is essentially the path from "I've *heard* that melody" to "I *know* that melody"; the path from receiving the melody to carrying and teaching the melody. Jewish musicians were often called *Klezmorim,* from the Hebrew "Klei - Zemer", meaning 'vessels of song', because they were the people who carried the songs around with them. Whether we play instruments or not, we can all strive to become vessels of the song, rather than musical bystanders, regardless of our formal musical background.

1. exposure   2. sing along with others

3. how does it start?   4. know it, sing it, teach it

Gold's 4-step Path to Melody Acquisition

1. Exposure: Every time we learn a melody, it's because we've put ourselves in a place where we can hear the melody. But this isn't just about hearing the melody, it's about noticing the melody, liking it, and wanting to be able to sing it. We may hear other melodies and we don't feel a particular attachment to them, but this particular one caught our ear.

The first hearing of a melody can be very powerful spiritually and emotionally, like the beginning of a relationship with a new friend or partner, and we need to let it ripple through us, because the same melody may take a while to feel that powerful again. This is the first date, or the honeymoon, before the long-term relationship really sets in, which has its own sets of rewards and challenges.

At the same time, melodies also come with baggage; they conjure up in us a host of emotional associations, and that's to be expected. The very same melody might seem exciting, boring, happy, or dreadful, depending on where a person has heard similar melodies or singing styles before. For example, once, after a singing session, somebody said to me, "I love that melody – it reminds me of my childhood cantor," and then three minutes later, another person told me, "You know, I hated that melody – it reminded me of my childhood cantor."

All of this goes to show that any melody can be good or bad depending on our past and our mood at present; in some ways, that takes the pressure off the melody! Since any melody can be good or bad, what's important is not what the melody is, but *how you sing it*.

2. Singing Along: In this second phase, you can sing along with the melody, as long as other people are really carrying the tune. Here's where patience becomes important. Everybody has different musical learning styles and abilities. For example, some will take a very long time to learn the melody, but eventually get it firmly in their minds, whereas others will very quickly "learn" the melody, and then promptly forget it. While some people seem to be able to sing along to a melody almost immediately, it really takes **at least twenty times** singing a melody before it really gets into the *kishkes* - before it's really internalized. So, sing along intentionally and try to catch a new part each time you hear it.

If you have a very musical ear that loves to harmonize, you might have to strictly avoid singing harmonies so that it doesn't become a secret tactic for avoiding learning the melody. My rule is: **No harmony** until you know the melody well enough to teach it.

With regards to words and text, again, everybody has different strengths. For example, some people have an easier time learning *nigunim* (melodies without words), because they find that trying to say the words correctly gets in the way of learning and ultimately singing the melody. Others find it impossible to remember all the twists and turns of a melody "in the air" unless they have words to hang the melody on, and they feel that the melody helps them to understand the words better. Whatever your strength, remember to have patience and sing the melody many, many times.

3. All But The Beginning: Here's the typical situation: in your minds' eye you're sure you could sing a whole, beautiful melody you've heard lots of times before and love – if you could just could remember the first three notes! It's always frustrating when you sit down to sing a song that you know is bound to be great, but you just can't seem to summon up how it starts!

"I could sing you a beautiful melody...if I could just remember...how it started"

To get past this stage, you'll have to practice remembering the beginning. Try to do things that make you forget the melody like singing another melody and then coming back to it, so that you're forced to try to remember the beginning without any clues. Use whatever musical tools you have in your bag. For example, does it help you to remember that the song is in minor, in 3/4 time, or has two pickup notes before the main beat? [5] Or, does remembering that the rhythm starts with a "ba-bump," or that you would tend to do a skip step when dancing to it, help? If you know about musical scales, you can memorize the numbers of the first few notes, such as "Low 5, 1, 2, 3..." The more musical elements you *notice* while singing it, the more *reminders* you can call upon when you're trying to access your memory banks as to how the darn thing starts.

4. Ready to Teach and Explore: When you know the melody, and can start it with no prompt or lag-time, then you are ready to teach others the melody or lead a group of people in singing it. You want a melody to just seep out of you, with no effort at remembering what comes next. Then you really know it. This is an exciting place to be with a melody, because then you can think about other musically expressive elements, like "how fast?" or "how loud?" or "how much ornamentation?" or "how much harmony?" and then you've entered the infinite path of musical invention which can occur with any melody at its base.

Throughout this four-step process, remember to be patient, and allow lots of repetition. You need to sing a melody at least twenty times before it really gets into the *kishkes*. Focus on the melody itself until it's clear, and the rest will follow.

How to Sing a Melody 20 Times in a Row: Creating Spontaneous Variations, Improvisations, and Interpretations.

5

A letter – it depends how you read it; a melody – it depends how you sing it!
(A brivl - vi men leynt es; a nigun, vi men zingt im!) –I.L. Peretz [6]

I used to know only five melodies, and people thought I was a *nign* expert-but what was really happening was that I was good at continuously reinventing those same melodies over and over again. I would work them this way and that, sing them loudly and quietly, fast and slow, with *dreys* (turns) and straight, you name it. Thus, one melody could easily last 20 minutes or longer, (all the more so when other people were singing, too). It's enough to know only five melodies, or even one melody, as long as you know how to milk that melody for all it's worth.

The main purpose here is to turn off our 'channel switching urge,' to turn off that boredom instinct that says "the next thing will be better than this." Reality check: The next melody we feel duty-bound to sing is just as good or bad as the current one. So what's the rush? Rather, we'd do better to stay on the same melody for a while focusing, instead, on *how we're singing it,* and *what we're bringing to it that is going to keep it fresh and alive.*

Resist the urge to change channels

At a shabbos *tisch*, for example, after the meal, when the people around you start singing *zmirot*, don't rush to the next melody when the first hasn't "happened" yet. So many opportunities for spontaneous, engaged singing are missed as people race through the *bentsher* (book of Shabbat blessings), saying "do you know this song?", compulsively flipping pages and maybe singing a tune only once through, without settling into the beauty of it, the uniqueness of it, or even the pure joy of singing, period. Take your time. One melody sung well makes a bigger impact on all present than 15 sung poorly! This is like having a long, relaxed conversation in which you make a new friend, as opposed to having twenty quick, small-talk conversations with who-knows-who, never remembering their faces or names. Melodies become our good friends only when we take a breath and allow ourselves to engage for a while.

Many of my favorite musicians model this mode of exploring a finite number of melodies. After seeing renowned mandolinist and clarinetist Andy Statman performing the same set of 12 melodies for about the 25th time, I asked him what it was like to play the same melodies over and over again, and he pulled me aside and insisted, "you don't need hundreds of melodies, you just need to explore what you've got..." In the same vein, B.B. King, the great blues guitarist, routinely takes an entire solo with just one note, playing it over and over again with different shakes and attitudes.

Cantor Schall routinely declares, albeit a bit dismissively, that all Jewish melodies are basically the same, plus or minus a little twist here or there. He's right, insofar as they're all made of the same building blocks (a few Jewish scales, rhythms, and familiar phrases) just rearranged slightly. I hope this at least begins to convince you that there's not much need to be anywhere else than where you are right now with a tune. Instead, stay on this one, right here, whatever it is. Make a commitment to the moment. Change yourself, not the melody.

In that vein, the old (seemingly boring) melodies are basically just as good as new (fresh and exciting) ones, and vice versa! Melodies can be *old friends* with whom you have a long, lovely history, or *new friends* with whom you get the excitement of the new encounter. New melodies can create fresh energy in the short term, as they come free of baggage and allow you to hear more purely. But what's really "fresh" in that situation is not the melody itself, but the attention you're giving it. The most creative singers know how to take that "fresh attention" and bestow it on the old chestnut melodies, and then we all rediscover that the boring old melodies are actually gems themselves! As the great Yiddish author and playwright, I.L. Peretz, writes:

> *"And a melody lives, and a melody dies, and a melody is forgotten as one forgets the dead! The tune was once young and vigorous! It was bursting with new life. After a time it became weaker; it outlived its time and lost its strength; it was over and done with; then its last breath dissipated in the air and suffocated somewhere, and it no longer existed!*
>
> *But a song can also be resurrected! (nor a nigun ken oyfshteyn tkhies hameysim)!*
>
> *Suddenly someone recalls an old melody. It suddenly emerges and bursts out of your mouth. Unintentionally one adds to it a new feeling, a new spirit, and it's almost as though a new melody has come alive. Now that's what we call the metamorphosis of a melody (a gilgul fun a nign)."* [7]

While this concept occurs with a melody over the course of hundreds of years, it also occurs in the span of two minutes; as a melody comes around to be started again, there's the opportunity to refresh the melody and sing it another twenty times.

So, following is a quick list of musical characteristics to consider that will help open up a melody each time it comes around:

Improvisational Concepts for a *Nign* [8]
1. Dynamics/Volume: how loud or soft do you want the notes to be? Screaming? Whispering?
2. Attack/Termination: how does each note start and end? Starting with different hard/soft syllables produces different effects, i.e., ta-ta-di-dah.... vs. ah-yah-yah-yah...., etc. Similarly, the ending of each note is also important to consider, as in a hard quick "taht" vs. an open-mouthed "tah." Ascertain: is a note accented?
3. Length of note: for how long does it sustain? Look for short notes vs. long notes.
4. Timbre/Tone: consider what the note sounds like coming through your voice. Is it a deep throated growl, or a sweet falsetto? Clean or Gritty? Is it operatic, or spoken?
5. Tempo/Rhythm: is the note in time, or out of time-is it emphasizing the rhythm, or 'floating' above it? Is it phrased ahead of the beat, on the beat, or behind the beat? Can you dance to it?
6. Ornaments/Note-frequency/Density: are there lots of extra little grace notes, slides,

trills, bends, scoops, kvetches, mordants – or none at all? Is it just a pure note?

7. Space: how much silence/how many rests are in between each note?
8. Contrast/context: how does each note compare to the other notes that come before and after?
9. Harmony: how does the note sound as various musical intervals are sung against it? Does the note sound consonant or dissonant?
10. Feeling/Emotion: what mood are you trying to convey? Yearning? Contentment? Or do we all just need to get up and dance?

Interpreting a Melody: Finding Its Structure, and Adding Ornaments

From a strictly melodic perspective, there are two directions to interpreting a melody: Taking notes out, and adding notes in. When you take enough notes out, you are left only with the structure of the melody, just as removing the walls from a house would leave you with only the foundational beams for structure, or, in our case, the skeleton of the melody. Once you've stripped away the melody to its barest bones, however, the melody suddenly becomes very spacious, and you find there is even more room for creativity. This is the "structural approach" to improvisation.

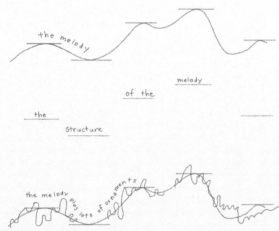

To imagine the structure of a melody, imagine hearing a group of singers across a lake, or a brass band in the distance: the details recede, but the ups and downs and beautiful mass of sounds remain, leaving room for your imagination to fill in some of the musical details.

The opposite approach is to take a melody and dress it up with all kinds of extra elaborations, adding vocal slides and ornaments and gussying it up. To use our previous analogies, this is like taking a basic house and putting lots of interesting paintings on the walls. Ornaments themselves are infinitely subject to improvisation, providing a good opportunity for *chazzonim* and singers who love to work at the fine-detail level of music.

The neat thing is that a group of people can go in both directions at the same time. Some simplify the melody and create a sort of *'ostinato'* (repeating bass-line) pattern, while others improvise melodic variations that work with the structure or sing the melody itself with lots of ornaments. In that way, a common, simple melody becomes the *ostinato* chordal comp for artistic coloratura that happens over the melody.

Basic Jewish Music Theory 6

*(Note: Some of the material in this chapter will be beyond beginner level.
Feel free to skip this chapter and come back to it later.)*

Studying music theory – the technical details of how music works – can help you remember melodies, and sing with greater confidence and authority. But some ask, "Does the mysterious, mystical quality of music disappear as you understand it more?" In my experience, that mysterious musical quality does sometimes disappear as you analyze the musical mechanics, but that's only temporary, for it comes back later on as a much deeper mystery, like the process of studying the cells of the human body ultimately increases one's wonder at the mysterious existence of life.

Following is a quick glance at the scales, rhythms, and harmonies that can be helpful to know about when creating your "Spontaneous Jewish Choir." These are only basic introductions, but I hope they'll get you started. Keep in mind that the feeling and style of this music (or any music) can take years to assimilate. Get out there and sing, and the understanding will gradually follow!

Scales (Modes)

Basic Scale Material: Most Jewish melodies are composed from sets of notes known as scales (or "modes" [9]). Singing up and down a scale is a basic melody in its own right. Learning the following five scales will help you understand just about any melody that you hear in most American shuls. [10] Initially, you'll ask yourself "what scale is this song in?", but eventually, with careful study, you will be able to say, "The first part of that song is in minor, but the second half it switches into *Freygish* (like the Greek phrygian scale) ..." If any of these details are tricky, remember to find yourself a good teacher!

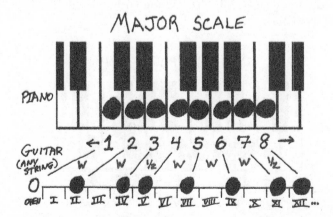

Every scale can be taught as a series of numbers (often 1-7). Sing up a major scale saying "1 (do) ... 2 (re) ... 3 (mi) ... 4 (fa) ... 5 (sol) ... 6 (la) ... 7 (ti) ... 8 (do again), 7,6,5,4,3,2,1..." Play it at the piano using the white keys from C to C to help you. That's MAJOR. It's the sound of the Torah Service, and the final Kaddish, and the Amidah.

Notice the distance between notes, what we call its "formula." In major, the formula is Whole Step, Whole Step, Half Step, Whole Step, Whole Step, Whole Step, Half Step, which is more easily written W W 1/2 W W W 1/2. Look at the diagrams to find the formulas for each scale. The other four scales will be described compared to the MAJOR scale, as follows:

1. MINOR: Flat [11] the 3,6, and 7 from the major scale, and you've got a MINOR scale (the notes are lower, hence "minor"). it's 1,2,b3,4,5,b6,b7,8. Think about the first five notes of "Hatikvah" to get hear the beginning of the minor scale. Sometimes the 7 is sharp, called "Harmonic Minor." Some *ba'alei tfilah* and musicians create powerful effects by flattening the 5 and 2 in special cases.

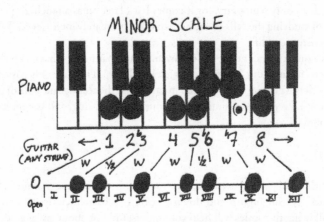

2. JEWISH MAJOR (or 'ADONAI MALACH'): Flat the 7 in the higher octave (often the low 7, below the 1 remains sharpened), and you've got "Jewish Major." It's 1,2,3,4,5,6,b7, as heard in Kabbalat Shabbat. When singing from 5-4-5, the 4 is often sharpened, resulting in 5-#4-5. Sometimes, when singing really high, a cantor might sing a flattened 10th on top, which is especially powerful!

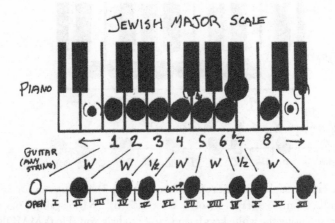

3. *FREYGISH* (or 'AHAVA RABA'): Flat the 2, 6 and 7, and you've got *FREYGISH*; [12] (remember, the 3 stays "major"). It's 1,b2,3,4,5,b6,b7,8. Remember to look in the diagrams for the formulas. Think "Avinu Malkeinu" or "Hava Nagilah" to get the sound in your head. It's used in prayer starting near the paragraph "Ahava Raba" in *Shacharit*, so it is often called the "Ahava Raba Scale."

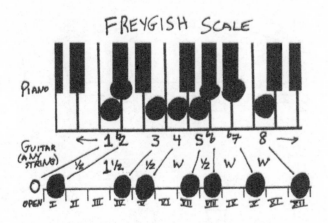

4. *MISHEBERACH* ('UKRAINIAN DORIAN', or 'DORIAN #4'): Flat the 3 and 7, and *SHARP* the 4, and you've got Misheberach. It's 1,2,b3,#4,5,6,b7,8. Many cantors use this scale during particularly pleading moments in the High Holiday liturgy.

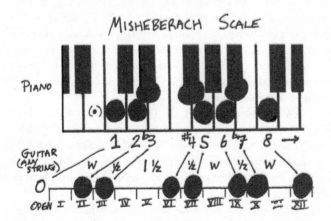

To make use of this information, ask some of the following questions when you hear a new melody: What scale is the song in? What number of the scale does the song start on? (It usually ends on 1, but often it may start on a different number, such as LOW 5). Are there any changes to the scale throughout the melody?

Rhythm!

The Downbeat: In any rhythm, the most important thing to know is the "downbeat," which is where you would count "**1**". This is the beat where everybody must come back together in a unified "stomp."

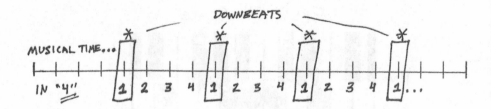

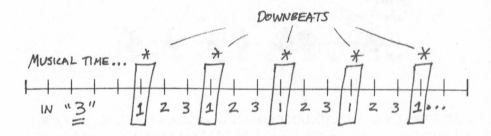

Melodies in 4 and 3: When trying to find the downbeat, the first question to ask yourself is, "What meter is this melody in-is it in 4, or is it in 3?" If you're "in 4", you'll count 1,2,3,4,1,2,3,4, giving an extra stomp (or accent) every 1st-of-4 beats. In three, often called a waltz, it will sound like 1,2,3,1,2,3. Often the faster dance melodies are in 4, whereas slower melodies are often waltzes (i.e., in 3).[13] You may be able to quickly figure out the beat. But, now, can you stomp on the downbeats with your foot, and slap the smaller beats with your hand on your knee, all while while singing a *nign*?

A few variations in 4 - "Debka," and "3,3,2": There are dozens of possibilities for variations of 3 and 4. Let's focus on a just a few variations on rhythms in 4. The "debka" rhythm can be felt by saying "**Dum** tek + tek **dum** + tek +" ("+" is a silent placeholder), creating the sort of syncopated Arabic feeling that shows up in so much Jewish music today. Remember, these rhythms may seem simple on their own, but try maintaining a melody while you hold down that beat with your feet and hands!

Another important rhythm to practice is the 3,3,2 rhythm (which is still in 4), where you count "1,2,3,1,2,3,1,2" and accent the "1's." To get this, you can also say out loud "long, long, short - long, long short" and so forth. There are two types of this rhythm. If you do it very fast it will have an African rhythmic feel, fast and syncopated. If you do it slow, it's a very open and subtly syncopated rhythm, closer to the old Jewish rhythms like the *freylakhs* and *bulgars* (fast Jewish rhythms) that Jews have danced to for centuries. It's twin brother is the 6,6,4 rhythm, which is the same thing doubled: 1,2,3,4,5,6,1,2,3,4,5,6,1,2,3,4. This rhythm has a great "open feel" to it.

Hadar Nign

Joey Weisenberg

Hearing the Rhythm in the Melody Alone: While these rhythms sound great when they're clapped or stomped, ultimately their accents should should be heard in the melody, itself. In other words, the rhythm gradually infiltrates the sung melody itself, with proper accents, so that you can hear the rhythm without the help of the clapping. To be sure, the voice alone can convey great rhythm!

Eliyahu Hanavi

Adapted from N. Vinaver

Rubber-band Melodies: Here are some examples of what I call Rubber-band Melodies: they're not in time, so you can "stretch" out certain parts in one direction or another. They tend to be more introspective, and afford lots of room for interpretation. When they have no words, these are often called *dveykus nigns* ("clinging to..." melodies), or *hislav'vus nigns* ("burning" melodies). This version of Eliyahu Hanavi is an example of a Rubber-band melody – as each time you sing it, you can elongate different notes.

Rhythmic subtleties

Danceability and "Lift": Rhythm ought to have a sense of "lift" to it – that unmistakable feeling that makes you sit up, and gets your tush to part from the chair. It urges you upwards, makes you instinctively want to dance. Rhythms should suggest dancing, even if people don't actually follow through. Your rhythm is succeeding if you look around the room and see people tapping their feet (and perhaps not even noticing).

Tempo: Let Slow be Slow! It is very hard to avoid speeding up while singing a melody. People get excited, and it naturally speeds up. But we've gotten to the point where many of us have never experienced singing slowly, or even at a medium tempo. One teacher of mine

What's your hurry? It's a nign, not a race.

jokingly claims that he remembers the exact moment in 1983 when Jews started speeding up. When singing a medium-tempoed piece, let it be medium! When singing slow, let it be slow! When singing fast, let it be fast! If you're going to speed up, at least speed up intentionally, after a medium-paced melody has had a nice long opportunity to be 'medium.'

Opening Up the Rhythmic Feel: Often, when there is lots of clapping or other sharp percussive sounds, there is less room for subtle vocal creativity.

Notice the effect of lots of hits versus fewer hits, and consider creating space by letting accents fall less frequently. In other words, the same tempo can feel jam-packed and dense, or vast and spacious, by increasing or decreasing the amount that you clap. One typical example would be "opening up" a waltz into a slow 6/8 beat, so that the accents fall only every other measure, giving a more spacious feel.

Phrasing in Between the Downbeats: Some people might be more relaxed in their singing, others more rushed, but everybody must come together at the beginning of each measure (or at least agree musically on exactly where the downbeat is, even if they're not singing on it). Keep your ears open for this beautifully elastic phenomenon found within Jewish music – a long, stretched-out measure of chaotic discord, followed by a unified down-beat. [14]

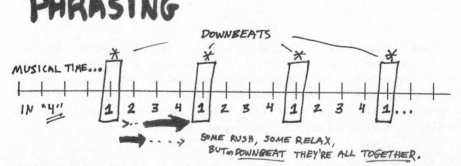

Rhythms with "Limps": There are some specific rhythmic feels that fall somewhere between metered and free: these are rhythms with "limps." This means that right before you hit the end of a bar, you hesitate just slightly before the downbeat. Doing this lends the rhythm a suspended feel, but involves a lot of paying attention on the part of everyone singing, because the rhythm is suddenly not entirely predictable.

Harmony

Jewish tradition is packed with harmony. Consider this story about how a famous cantor refused to sing without his bass singer's harmonic support:

> "... Some time after his visit in Lizhensk, [the cantor of the famous Ba'al Shem Tov] lay down and died. Thirty days after that, and again on a Friday, the bass singer came from the mikveh (bath of purification) and said to his wife: "Summon the chevre kadisha (Holy Brotherhood) quickly to see to my burial, for in paradise they have commissioned my cantor to sing for kabbalat shabbat, and he does not want to do that without me. "He lay down and died." [15]

Harmony happens in two forms: spontaneously improvised harmony, and through-composed harmony. One historian/composer describes the spontaneous, improvised nature of harmony singers of the 18th century:

> "... choirs, consisting of the best the ghetto had to offer, followed the improvisations of the cantor with instinctively felt harmonies, often in 4 parts. A bass was often required to improvise on the spot, a sort of prologue or overture before the selection proper, and it was not unusual for the alto to accompany the newly improvised tune of the Cantor a sixth below, or for any member of the choir to join in the singing of the original melody." [16]

By the end of the 19th century, and mostly in Germany, composers such as Solomon Sulzer (1804-1890) and Louis Lewandowsky (1821-1894) felt the need to keep up with the church by creating four-part through-composed settings of the liturgy, settings that "with solos, choral numbers, and responses in modern form... brought order into the hitherto chaotic profession." [17]

If you are able to summon enough music-reading singers to sing complex choral music, the results will undoubtedly be amazing. In lieu of that, however, don't be afraid to make good use of the spontaneous harmonies that people who are untrained, yet naturally musical, still manage to sing intuitively. There can be one harmony, or two, or three or as many as you like. Here are a few different basic harmonic ideas to experiment with:

1. Octaves: simply having people sing in higher and lower octaves fattens up the melody dramatically.

2. Parallel harmonies: a third above, a sixth below, or sometimes a third below, moving up and down, parallel with the melody.

3. Static notes: often forming the third part of the harmony, these notes change less fre-

quently than the melody, but fill in the gaps above, below, or in between the melody and the parallel harmony to form three part chords.

4. Bass notes: a low singer can sing the notes that form, for example, the roots of chords.

5. Simple Counterpoint: for example, to make a "mirror" counterpoint, sing a line that goes down when the melody goes up, or vice versa.

Cautions with Harmony:
Here are a few rules for allowing harmony to be helpful and not counterproductive:

- Don't use harmony as a crutch for not learning melody.

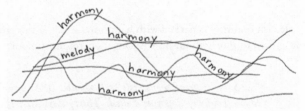

Too many harmony lines obscure a melody line.

- Wait to sing harmonies until the melody has had a chance to warm up and develop, i.e., let it come in as a beautiful addition later, not as something from the very beginning.

- Don't let the melody get lost in a huge wash of chordal sound. The melody is primary. Stick to parallel harmonies first, until you're sure the contour of the melody is being maintained by the room.

- Finally, like in blues singing, there is room for some "dirtiness" and unplanned dissonance. Jewish singing does not have to imitate a classical or church choir. Some of the old klezmer band recordings would sound dirty and unpolished, but hauntingly beautiful. That said, strive for unity.

Part III

Teaching and Leading Jewish Music

Breishit Rikud Nign

Joey Weisenberg

Karcigar Nign

Joey Weisenberg

Teaching Melodies: A Practical, Stand-Alone Class 7

In order to have a singing community, there's no doubt about it: somebody needs to start teaching melodies. If you know a melody, teach it to a friend. If you know a lot of melodies, start teaching classes to groups of people! **In the same way that we all must find teachers, we must all become teachers, and enter into the cycle of learning and teaching that fosters communal development.** In this section, I'd like to empower you to become proficient and confident teachers of Jewish song. It's practical advice, time-tested and hard-won after I've spent numerous hours teaching melodies in shuls and have arrived at what I consider to be a formula that works. I try to keep my goals simple and actionable. Remember that the most important goal for a music teacher is to **communicate a love for music**, and to thereby teach others to love and engage positively with music too.

Teaching melodies

Most broadly speaking, to be this sort of teacher, you'll need to keep in mind, and create in your students, three basic proficiencies: 1) Know the material well enough yourself that you can ably demonstrate it; 2) Get the participants to the point where they know the material so well that they eventually won't need you as facilitator; and 3) Encourage at least some of the students to start teaching others. This won't require that you have oodles of music theory or an education degree under your belt, at least in a shul setting, so take heart. But you will need a certain amount of personal conviction, and awareness. Why?

Because as much as we're trying to pave the way for learning and teaching in the future, we can't forget about taking the time to experience the power of music together, in class, RIGHT NOW! We must create real moments right now, moments which will, believe it or not, inspire real moments in the future. It's incumbent upon us as singing teachers to find the power to be present, even in the midst of a diverse group. **As one of my teachers put it, "Stop preparing to be a musician, and start being a musician right now..."**

The following is a detailed description of a class that I've taught, and that I would recommend you teach. Its end goal is to create a "Spontaneous Jewish Choir" in real time, using the skills of people of all backgrounds, ages, and experience levels. (And YES, it is possible!) First a brief USER'S GUIDE: I've divided my instructions into sections, based on what needs to happen (and when) – along with common questions. I use italics to mark those actions that I am doing physically, as well as phrases or instructions that I am saying out loud to the class; the rest of the text will provide you with pedagogical notes, or at least let you know what you ought to consider while the class is happening in real time.

Enjoy!! I think you'll find facilitating Jewish music to be one of the most rewarding teaching experiences there is.

SJC (SPONTANEOUS JEWISH CHOIRS): THE PRACTICUM

WHERE TO BEGIN

Afford yourself some **Pre-Class Preparation time**. It will pay off. Sit in a quiet space for a while, and dream up melodies that you love. You're going to have to like the melody you're teaching, or you won't be convincing as a teacher. **Prepare three melodies** of different tempos and styles. Of those three, you'll only actually teach one, which will be the one that makes sense when you actually encounter the students and see what kind of mood everybody's in. Pick the one that you think you're going to do and sing it to yourself, at least enough to make sure that you know its structure and, most importantly, how it starts.

Sing the melody to yourself quietly.

Review various aspects of that melody...Are you sure what kind of melody it is? Is it in major or minor? What's its rhythm? Have you sung it yourself 20 times (the minimum to really know it)? Have you created your own spontaneous variations on it? [18] Have you internalized it? Ideally, you should have a thorough understanding of all the theoretical elements that surround the melody, so that you're prepared to 'think on your feet' and give helpful answers when put on the spot. However, if you don't know every single theoretical detail, and you only know the melody, don't let it stop you – go ahead and teach music! Only, do consider catching up on the musical background over the coming weeks, months, and years. (Sometimes teaching a classes can actually kickstart this deeper exploration for yourself. That's one of the unsung benefits of teaching music: Learning!)

OK, I'M READY.
WHERE DO I TEACH? WHAT MAKES THE BEST SINGING-CLASSROOM?

Let me preface my instructions to you here by saying first that I believe that a good space can play just as important role in your teaching success as a good song. Hence:

Find the **smallest possible room** that will accommodate the expected number of students. Just as we described the effects of close singing-davenning, a singing class will be far more powerful when it is set up to be very **focused**. [19] You may have to specially request a small room ahead of time, depending upon where you're teaching.

Set up no more than four chairs, in a circle.

I call this small circle my **"Chair Trick,"** and with it, I effectively lower expectations and increase the success of class. With only a few chairs set up, you immediately telegraph to anyone who enters that a small class is a good class.

As people come in, say something like the following:
"This is going to be wonderful! We four people get to sing together!"

The psychology behind this is: Our class is going to be good with four people – so all the better if more show up! The message that you send with this kind of attitude is "This will be awesome even if we're a very small group." Numbers don't matter as much as enthusiasm, focus, and energy. If you set up 30 chairs, and only eight people come in, the circle will feel empty and inadequate. But if you set up four chairs and eight come in, the class feels enormously successful right off the bat! *"Wow, even more people came than we expected! Double the expectations!!!"*. What's most important for you, as a budding teacher, is that you project good energy and confidence as the class gets started, and this chair trick helps you to feel like things are working. **Always strive to communicate contentment with the current situation, not desperation.**

Pull chairs outward to expand the circle, and add chairs as more people come in.

The Chair Trick...put only a few chairs out at first, then expand as people come into the room, so the circle always feels full!

It may seem like an interruption to move chairs once the class has started, but pulling back chairs makes people feel like they're doing a good deed, and also helps acknowledge each person who comes in, which, in turn, makes each person feel more special.

Until there are over 20 people, make sure everybody sits in the front row by only having one row of chairs in a circle. That way nobody has the option sit in the back talking, merely observing, or pretending like they're not there. You have to set up the room for success, and this means only leaving open the options that will work towards the goal of people singing with you. Yes, it's micromanaging. But well worth it, when you consider all of the difficulty in getting people to sing!

Mess up the chairs.

In general, wherever you lead or teach a group, you should mess up the chairs a little.

Whenever I go into a chapel, I run around the room messing up the chairs, pulling one sideways, another out of line. Straight chairs mean straight behavior; they send a tacit message to people that they ought to keep their emotions "in line" too, that creative and improvisational behavior will be far from rewarded. I also like to use **messing up the chairs** as my way of getting familiar with the room, learning about the geometry and acoustics of it as I *patchke* around the space. Another, added benefit of this chair unstraightening activity is that it can also be communal: when early-arrivals show, I ask them to help, and invariably, they have fun, and immediately start to feel a part of things.

NOW THAT WE'RE ALL HERE, WHAT DO WE DO?

Start with a warm-up melody, as people are coming in, even before you talk.

Pick a wordless melody that you think people know and like: something peaceful, not too slow or too fast. One example might be a *nign* version of a well-known liturgical moment – like *"Yism'chu,"* [20] without the words. Never start by talking; it kills the energy and makes people think a lecture is what they're in store for (NOOOOO!). As people are singing, take the opportunity to look around the room and see who is there. Do you know them? What are their names? Inch your chair in toward the center, encouraging others to do the same, so that people get used to being closer together right away. After completing four or five rounds of the melody, finish it off with a clear gesture, then introduce yourself and say:

"Thank you for coming and for having me here; this is going to be great!" And smile. [21]

Frame what you're about to do for the next hour and a quarter; give a short explanation ahead of time so people can understand the process of learning as it unfolds.

WHAT'S MY SINGING SYLLABUS GOING TO BE?

Now say to your group the following:
"We're going to learn one melody today, and sing it 20 times, until we really have explored it..."

Pick **one melody**, and focus on it for the entire hour. One melody is enough for a spectacular musical event. You don't need ten melodies, or even two. [22] My goal is to always treat the class as an opportunity to deeply experience and explore a melody, not to rush through a dozen.

Which melody should you pick? My first choice for teaching is always a melody that no one in the room yet knows. Why? This puts everybody on the same level, encourages everyone to fully experience the challenge to sing, in the moment, together; plus it's harder to imagine that you're boring someone when they don't know what's going to happen next. Sometimes I'll even go so far as to change my choice for a teaching melody at the last minute if someone walks in the room who I know already knows it.

Sing the whole melody through, start to finish.

People need to hear the entire melody in context, as a whole. When you sing it the first time, sing with confidence, and make it beautiful, so people can begin to forge a relationship with the melody. Then begin to do **call and response** with digestible chunks: one phrase at a time.

"Okay, now will you please repeat after me..." Sing a phrase, wait for response.

Do call and response **in time**. Keep the beat while teaching, so that the energy level stays up. Even when you take a moment to talk, see if you can tap your foot in time while you talk, so that you keep the flow going. This process of call and response learning can be very beautiful, rhythmic, and melodic in its own right, as long as continuity is maintained.

Repeat all the phrases until the first section of a melody is finished. Sing only that first section over and over again.

Before you stop and talk, make sure people have accomplished something really tangible, such as learning the first section of a melody all the way through, without prompting. If they know they've finished as much as half or a third of the song, they'll have the confidence to finish it. If you start talking too early, you'll derail the process with talk, and you'll have to get the energy flow started all over again from scratch. After you've finished the first section, however, **ask a few questions** to get more people involved.

"How does this melody seem to you? Hard?... Easy?" "How is this one... nice?"

Always ask questions, rather than telling people what to think. Of course, sometimes, you have to model the fact that you love the melody (for those who can't tell by your body language) by admitting, "Wow, that's beautiful." Look at people as they respond, and respond to their responses. Of course, while you're talking, you should also be doing your best to assess how much of the time spent talking is truly productive, and how much is diversion. Keep in mind that people will tend to want to talk rather than learn, so make sure to cut off the discussion well before the point at which everybody suddenly spaces out, and the energy you've worked so hard to generate in the room is lost. [23]

Sing and teach the next section of the melody.

Establish what the purpose of the melody is: Ask,

"What's this melody doing? What's its purpose?"

Weigh in with a quick explanation of various types of *nigunim: Dveykus nigns* and *rikud nigns,* for example, call up different moods and spiritual aspects.

Put the first two sections together, without stopping. Model the musical structure physically, for instance, by putting up two fingers when the second section is starting.

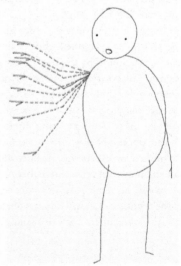

Conduct the rising and falling of pitch

Use your hands a lot; **conduct** the ups and downs of the melody. People who are not used to using their ears will value this visual reference.

I'M NOTICING THAT PEOPLE HAVE VASTLY DIFFERENT SKILL LEVELS. WHAT DO I DO?

No matter how clear you are, some people will have trouble initially; soon enough they'll burst out and despair: "I'll never remember this, it's too hard," or "I don't like this one," or "It doesn't fit the text..."

Remind people of your goals with simple coaching phrases like: *"It takes time and* **patience** *to learn a melody and make friends with it,"* or *"Sometimes a melody grows on you as it becomes more familiar."*

Help them to appreciate the complexity and depth of longer, more difficult melodies. Unfortunately, it's the tendency today to favor instantly predictable – and ultimately forgettable – melodies in favor of those that yield their rewards over time. Here, our goal is to re-learn what we might 'think' we already know; to absorb a melody more than just 'sing' it. In my opinion, the longer you spend with a really special *nign*, the better it gets.

The vast majority of people can learn melodies, even hard ones, even if they initially seem timid and say things like "I'm not a good singer." Be prepared, however. There are indeed some people who can't learn even the simplest melody, who don't have the ear, can't hold a tune. Have compassion for them – but don't let them off the hook; rather, find something at which they can succeed, like hitting their knee in time, or bobbing back and forth to the music meditatively. Involving the less-talented students requires enormous patience and creativity and tests your ability as a teacher. But don't forget about them!

You might want to look at these singing classes as though they were microcosms of the Jewish community at large: as such, you need to embrace the fact that people bring to the circle diverse and varied sets of skills, not to mention their hangups, preconceived stigmas, and incredibly rich insights. The most tone-deaf singer can turn out to be a clear and insightful liturgy teacher, once it comes time for the singing circle to switch to 'talk' mode. The trick is to keep everyone feeling challenged without embarrassment. On equal footing. And invaluable. Sound hard? It is, a bit, so here's the trick: you'll need to exercise your Just and Rightful Authority. (Diplomacy helps, too!) While you're observing your group, try to assess what people's skills are. Then (and yes, this may be difficult at first) push them in directions that are tough for them. For example, people who are very good at singing melodies may need lots of work on clapping rhythms, or people who are very good at singing harmonies on the spot might have a harder time concentrating enough to really learn the melody, start to finish. Don't let people do only what they are comfortable with, or they will start to space out and they won't come back, because they'll feel that they already know everything. Guide everybody just a bit past his or her comfort zone; if you can do this successfully, the beauty of the resulting nign will be everyone's reward. What's more, they'll want to come back to do it again (remember, that's also your goal!).

OK, MOST OF THE CLASS HAS BEGUN TO 'GET' IT! CAN WE START TO IMPROVISE?

Sing and teach the final section of the melody. Announce: "NO HARMONY UNTIL YOU KNOW THE ENTIRE MELODY WELL ENOUGH TO TEACH IT!"

I always have a standing rule in my singing sessions: **No harmony** until you know the entire melody. This helps everybody learn the melody better, as some people cannot learn melodies while harmonies are being sung, and conversely, some people harmonize as a subtle means of not focusing on really learning the melody. The melody is primary!

Sing again.

Once you've taught the entire melody, you're going to have to repeat it ad nauseum. **Repeat, repeat, repeat, repeat.** Repeat it at least 20 times throughout the class, if you want people to really learn it. Here's where your musical expertise and creativity are put to the test, as you'll need to find excuses to sing the melody over and over again, all of them different. One time you'll focus on dynamics (loud or soft), then next on rhythm, the next on staccato or legato syllables *("tai-di-dai vs lai-lai-lai")*, or focus on any other musical elements that come to you spontaneously as you teach. [24] Sing/talk/sing; patter/vamp/sing again as many times as possible. Meanwhile they'll be internalizing the melody and absorbing essential musical techniques.

HOW CAN I BRING THE GROUP TOGETHER, RHYTHMICALLY?

Now ask: "What's the rhythm of this song?"

Get to work on the rhythmic underpinnings of the music. Tell people to stomp their feet on the **downbeats,** and slap their knees on the 2's, 3's, and 4's, depending on the rhythm. Slapping the knee can be a good way to involve people who may not want to seem like they're dancing or clapping in any conspicuous way. Collectively determine what you've got here; is it a waltz, um-chuk, debka, 3-3-2 rhythm or a new rhythm that's being creatively invented on the spot?

Sometimes, in the course of trying to establish a group rhythm, the group as a whole will have a hard time finding just where to set the downbeat. At this point, you'll want to get people up off their tushes to do, what I call, the Downbeat Dance. [25]

Stomp forward with the right foot "1!!", rock back onto the left "2", right foot back "3", rock onto the left "4". Repeat. Sing the melody while dancing.

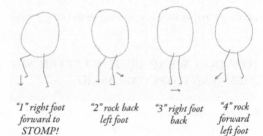

"1" right foot forward to STOMP!   *"2" rock back left foot*   *"3" right foot back*   *"4" rock forward left foot*

In between the beats, raise your hands or your shoulders to show the upbeats. Explain that the upbeats draw us proudly up, and make us want to rise up and transcend our situation, whereas the downbeats keep us firmly rooted in time and place. We stand in the middle dancing between heaven and earth.

HOW DO I ASSESS WHERE ALL THIS DANCING AND CLAPPING IS TAKING US MUSICALLY?

Stop dancing, keep singing: did the rhythm improve?

You should be able to stop the dancing, stop the foot/knee percussion, and stop the clapping, and still hear the rhythm from the voice alone! Encourage people to bring out all the rhythmic accents with their voices, and without the crutches of percussion.

Sing again. Is the tempo staying constant (ideal), or speeding up (more likely)?

See if you can maintain the *nign* at a slow or moderate (i.e., not-too-fast, not-too-slow) pace. Or, to make your point, try singing the entire melody super-fast, even in an exaggerated fast and funny way to illustrate how much more the melody "breathes" when it is kept moderate.

NOW WHAT: WHAT'S THE PRAYERFUL OUTCOME OF ALL THIS SONG?

*Sing it out for yet one more round; only this time stop to ask: "What do the **Words** mean?" (Conversation ensues)... "Does the music fit with the words? If it does, How? If not, Why not?"*

After this much musical work, it's often wise to take a break, sit back down, and switch to a more analytical, intellectual mode as a group. For many people, music is a great point of entry into a deeper understanding and connection to Hebrew text; it allows people to get the words or prayers more firmly implanted in their mouths and memories. Once you know how to say the words, you are in effect, already on the path to understanding what they mean, which, like learning music, is also a life-long pursuit. However, there's the constant debate to contend with, and you'll no doubt face it here:

"What's more important: the words, or the music?" The class members will probably want to raise this question here. Some will insist that the text is primary; that music is all about supporting the prayers. Others will point out that singing *nigunim* (which don't even have words) is one of the most spiritually uplifting things we ever get to do! Who is right? that's the ongoing dialog, isn't it? In the end, both are important, and hopefully support and nurture each other. Let the class get into the discussion here; it may just be the most rewarding part of all their efforts! Just make sure the talk doesn't go on too long. Before you know it, you'll lose that amazing, crackling-with-energy, musical vibe you've worked so hard to create.

HOW DO I WRAP UP THE EXPERIENCE IN A WAY THAT WILL MAKE THEM WANT TO COME BACK?

Ask, "How does that melody start?" Have someone else lead the melody.
And, believe it or not, sing again.

You've talked, and analyzed, and reflected. But, have you forgotten the tune? Maybe so! Laugh about it. Reassure them that this is to be expected. Reward anyone and everyone for remembering any part of the song they can. And laugh again: you may have forgotten it, yourself! Getting someone else to be the melody maven empowers them. Keep in mind: the hardest part is to remember the first three notes!

THE PAYOFF (QUIET, OR YOU MIGHT MISS IT)

Now that you've sung the melody 10-15 times, you'll find that people are **finally starting to "forget" that they are singing** and that somehow, without their realizing it, the music is starting to seep out of them in a more natural and beautiful way. Sometimes it's only after the 10th or 12th time around that people are truly warmed up and really singing effortlessly.

Sing again. Listen to the last note of each phrase. don't be afraid to draw it out, to make it beautiful. Take big breaths, make it last.

Often people will run out of air and stop singing before a note has had a chance to flourish. Suggest that people **'follow through'** to the ends of notes, and sing all the way until the very end of songs, so that the music doesn't seem like it is dying at the end of each musical sentence. Take big breaths, and follow through.

Sing again. When the very last bit of sound stops, leave a moment of **silence.**

The quieter it is after the song ends, the more powerful the melody will seem in retrospect. It's like leaving New York City for a day upstate in the mountains; the quiet gives you perspective on the sound, the contrast helps you appreciate each extreme more. Let the melody seem to resonate in the air this way. Just be aware that different groups of people have different capacities for silences: some people will start shifting in their chairs, doing anything to make noise so that it's not quiet. Some 'silence moments' will last only 10 seconds and seem like an eternity, while others will go on for minutes or longer and seem to end too soon. All of them are fine. Take the reflection time for yourself, too, and feel good about the group you've just formed.

AND NOW, FOR THE FINALE!

Everybody stands up and comes closer together. Sing again.

End every class **standing**. Bring people in, closer together than they were when sitting, and prepare for a good time, because the melody you've been working on for an hour will suddenly emerge in full force, and it becomes a wonderful climactic ending.

"Release the harmonies!"

We've avoided harmony for most of the class, partly to make it easier to learn the melody, and partly as a helpful pacing tool for a class. It lets things build up more slowly, so that when you end up standing together at the end of a class, and you say, "Okay, now let the harmonies out!" you end up with an amazing climax, an event that's suddenly doubled in intensity and beauty. You want this exponential increase of intensity at the very end of the class, so people leave feeling like they really just did something special.

Finish class three minutes early.

People should always be left longing for more; they should leave the room smiling and feeling good. If it's *Shabbat*, finish the *nign*, say 'Good shabbos!' and **end decisively with no extra talk.** If it's a regular weekday, just say "Thank you!" and decisively finish, and leave the circle. (That said, do your best to hang out in the room afterwards: people will appreciate having you around to answer their questions and hear their concerns.)

CONGRATULATIONS. MUSIC ACCOMPLISHED: YOU'VE CREATED A SPONTANEOUS JEWISH CHOIR IN REAL TIME!

END NOTES: MUSIC CLASS TROUBLESHOOTING

Yes, there are times when a class won't respond, despite all of your best efforts and preparation; you start to feel frustrated, depressed – sometimes almost debilitatingly so. You look at your watch and wonder how you're possibly going to get through the remaining hour of the class. Unfortunately, this is (if only occasionally) a very real part of the teaching process. Here are some things I tell myself, ways I coach myself through just such situations.

Stop. Take a breath. Stand up or sit down. Walk slowly over to the window and open it, asking people if they mind the air (maybe your simple, physical change of pace will elicit a much-needed, ice-breaking comment)... Quickly brainstorm. Improvise. Ask a question. Do anything to elicit a response from the group, but remember to stay in CONTROL of yourself. You don't want to embarrass anyone, or you'll compound the problem. Ask everybody "What are we doing here?" and wait five seconds for them to answer that question themselves. Let a difficult situation be a teaching moment for all by explaining that **the whole purpose of music is to engage,** *and that that's what we're trying to do here. Explain the 'tipping point of a room' idea,*[26] *and ask, point blank: "What do you think: Have we reached the tipping point yet?"*

If nothing results, just accept the situation. Smile – both because the room will certainly benefit from the much-needed positive energy, and because you can't win them all. Sometimes that exact moment you accept defeat and let go is the moment when the whole thing turns around and beauty emerges. Just try to smile and enjoy!

Leading Services: For the Beginner *Ba'al Tfilah* 8

This chapter will describe the path to becoming a *ba'al tfilah* (prayer leader) in your congregation or minyan, starting from the first steps. In Chapter 9, we'll look at concepts that apply to more experienced *ba'alei tfilah*.

Daven. Go to shul. See what it is you're getting into. The first step, like that of learning a melody, is exposure. You have to go to shul on a regular basis at least for a focused amount of time; you'll want to absorb the pacing and flow of the davenning, and listen to how others lead davenning and soak up their style. Before you can consider leading, you have to have lots of experience as a *kahal* davener, both so that you hear the *nusach* over and over again, and so that you know what it's like to BE LED. When you feel comfortable, start participating however you can, by singing along, saying enthusiastic "Amens," or bringing a positive energy to the room. Stand as close to the *ba'al tfilah* as possible, to pick up on as many nuances as possible, as well as to give that leader the support that you'll want eventually.

Whenever it's feasible, try to take advantage of the opportunity to attend a service that's vastly different from your own shul's. You will want to get an overview of different *minhagim* (local traditions), *siddurim* (prayer books), architectures of physical space, and styles. Perhaps there are a number of shuls from different backgrounds from your own in your area – Reform, Chasidic, Conservative, Modern Orthodox, Reconstructionist, Independent, Sephardic, Ashkenazic – and you simply haven't checked them out yet. Do so. Having a sense of the range of davenning experiences can both give you good ideas to bring to your own shul, and help you understand your own services better by means of contrast.

Find a *nusach* **teacher.** A PERSON. Websites, CD-roms, *nusach* books, and CD's: they're all great as resources, but nothing can substitute for a real-life teacher with whom you can interact in person. A person gives you a feeling of attachment to real tradition; plus you get the added bonus of all those quirky, funny, idiosyncratic details of getting to know someone that make life richer. Take, for example, my own beloved teacher, Cantor

Find a teacher

Schall: my studies with him weren't only about learning *nusach*. They were about going into his basement where the walls were literally covered with baseball-card-sized photos of famous cantors and rebbes, and seeing the cigar in Cantor Schall's left hand progressively blacken the left side of the piano while he played chords. It was about watching him pull out crumbling manuscripts that he had used as a teacher 60 years ago, hearing him scream into the telephone anytime someone called and interrupted us. When you learn traditions from living beings, the tradition becomes alive for you.

Along those lines, I'd suggest you seek out teachers from a broad range of ages and backgrounds. One teacher should be over eighty (or thereabouts), to give you a feel for the styles of previous generations. One should be closer in age to you, to help you understand what is in fashion today (though of course what's in fashion is not necessarily better! Still, it's really helpful to know). In the last few years, for example, I've learned dozens of cantorial recitatives (their stylings too complex to ever use in normal davenning), while at the same time, I gleaned tones of great melodies from friends and peers – the sort of fare I can use and sing in public at a dinner table, the very same night. That said, all the beautiful *chazzones* (cantorial music) my older teacher shared with me I've now absorbed more than mastered; it's such a part of my music-prayer vocabulary at this point, I wouldn't, and couldn't, trade my "old-school" instruction for anything. It's thanks to teachers like Cantor Schall that we can get a deep sense of continuity with prayerful attitudes of the past.

Depending on where you live and other factors, it's not always easy to find a good teacher. But keep your eyes open, and ask around. If you're consciously looking for teachers, then you'll be ready to seize the moment when the teacher appears.

Make recordings for yourself. Record your lessons; play them back frequently, until you memorize the *nusach* and melodies.

Get it in writing. Ask your teachers if they have the music written down, as reading the music can help you get a better sense of its structure. If you don't read music, then why not start now! Transcribing the music yourself is also very helpful; it really forces you to process the music thoroughly and notice musical nuances. However, while recordings, written music, and personal transcriptions from your teacher are essential, ultimately there will come a point where you have to put all the media away, have the music memorized, and daven straight from the *siddur*.

Learn the *nusach*, then apply it to text. Differentiate between *nusach* and melodies. *Nusach* is the free-flowing musical pattern that is sung solo by the *ba'al tfilah*, that changes in different sections of the service. Melodies are sung usually in only one place, are rhythmic, and, most importantly, *melodies are the parts where, generally, everybody else sings along*.

As you learn *nusach*, pay attention to how the *nusach* changes for different services: Thanks to *nusach*, Jewish prayer has the power to – quite literally – tell time with song; learn the proper *nusach*, sing it with confidence with the text, and you will give the congregation an immediate snapshot of the time of year, time of week, all the way down to the time of day. For example, by just listening to the way the *chazzan* chants the *half-kaddish*, we are reminded that it is Rosh Hashana morning, or Sukkot evening, or *shabbat* afternoon, or many other times of the Jewish year. Funny, but the more specific we are in shul with our prayer, timewise, the more time seems to stand still, and our ancient past catches up with us. Being a keeper of this continuum is very special, and *nusach* is one of the keys.

That's right, there are sixteen different versions of the Half-Kaddish that are sung throughout the Jewish year, demonstrating the different *nusachs* that one must know to lead all the services. But you don't need to know all of them in order to get started. Pick one service, and learn it well, and the others will follow!

To get started, find the beginning of a service, and carefully study the *nusach* for that piece of text. Usually, you can learn one 'paradigm *nusach*' that will apply to all the other following text in a given section. For example, learn "L'chu N'ran'na" (psalm 95) very carefully, and you'll have learned eighty percent of the musical material you need to finish Kabbalat *Shabbat*. Learn "Shochen Ad" carefully, and you'll get your ears tuned up for the first section of *shabbat Shacharit*. Learn "L'Dor Vador" carefully, and your voice will be ready for the rest of the *Amidah* from that point on. The point is, small bits of musical *nusach* can take you through many pages of liturgy, but you need to make sure you learn the initial paradigms well.

Once you've learned the initial *nusach* of a section, move on to applying it to the rest of the text. Most prayerbooks will have a little box or symbol that tells you which text you need to say out loud. Most always it will cue you to come in at one or two sentences before the end of each paragraph. Also, when I'm learning to chant new prayer-texts, I almost always **locate the logical breaks** in every sentence, and then insert commas and visible vertical lines in between clauses, to remind myself where to start and stop and how to phrase the words. If your Hebrew skills aren't perfect, consider using a *siddur* 27 that breaks up the sentences and translates every word and phrase, so that you can quickly see the logical breaks.

If you have enough time, you may want to **learn a specific setting** for each part that you're going to say – i.e, learn to sing it *exactly* the way your teacher does it. While it takes much more time to learn, it also gives you a much deeper connection to every word, as well as the confidence that you really know the material start to finish. Even if you've learned this way – the long way – you can still use a more improvisatory approach later, but at least you'll have a set version you can always fall back on.

Practice transitions, and "call and response" sections. Practice every word that you'll have to say out loud, over and over again, in a quiet place, so you can hear yourself making mistakes.

Now, as you get more confident with most of the prayers, you'll want to focus on practicing *transitions* between sections. Master the transitions, and you'll feel truly confident and better prepared. Why? Simply put, transitions are like the gaps between the building blocks, the space between the bridge and the paved road. It's easy to stumble, lose your way as you have to change musical modes (say from minor to *freygish*), 28 or when you have to remember a *nusach* after a communal melody, or lead the entire congregation into a huge, popular, singalong melody that everyone knows – like when the service suddenly transitions from minor key to major in preparation for a resounding (and decidedly major) *"Shema Yisroel."*

Pay special attention to the words that you utter, as *ba'al tefilah*, directly before the congregation responds with a resounding 'AMEN', or the like. These are yet another kind of transition, between solo voice and group voice. They come often, and, if you can master these transitional moments, you'll find they make for a more satisfying aura of group prayer. For example, say *"V'imru"* very strongly to clearly cue the congregation to say "Amen," and leave a deliberate space after you start a *bracha* (blessing) *'Baruch ata ado---,'* for people to say *"Baruch Hu U'va'ruch Sh'mo."* If you are not sure exactly where these moments are, consult with a rabbi, and also check in a *siddur* with detailed instructions. 29

Study the language and meanings of the prayers, but keep moving forward in your leadership skills, even if it means glossing over some of the textual details. Ideally, we would all know the meaning (and maybe several interpretations of) each word we're saying. The liturgy is an ever-expanding source of beautiful imagery, analogies, ideas, structures, and inspiration. Ahh, if we were all scholars! But in reality, it may make more sense to employ whatever skills we have already, start leading, and allow ourselves to learn more about the text throughout the years, as we go. One needn't be a master of the Hebrew language to lead, but that said, one should know the basic idea of each thing he's saying, and feel oneself to be on the path towards learning and understanding more of the words. [30] Some would argue that the main point of music is to serve the words. In my view, however, words are only one part of of the bigger picture. Prayer texts, singing, movement, and meditation all work together to serve the greater goal of appreciating and responding to the wondrous and divine nature of the world around us. This is what it means to have a relationship with *Hakadosh Baruch Hu*. When you lead a service, you're creating a *tam* – literally, 'a taste' of holiness, that puts us in touch with our traditions, communities, and personal intentions; I'd argue that it's this *tam* that truly allows us to realize the greater purpose of prayer. A multi-dimensional davenning experience should re-enliven our sense of worldly wonder, and thereby give us the spiritual strength to treat that world with decency and respect.

Rehearse in front of your teacher, or other friends who will give you honest feedback. Sing into a tape recorder or your computer, and then listen back. Analyze your continuity. Flow. Fluency. Attitude. Pronunciation. What is the overall feeling? Do I sound competent? Continuity is the main thing. Time yourself. How much time do you have to finish a service? Did you make it? If no, practice saying the words more fluently. Prepare yourself so you can say the words very quickly, at light-speed if necessary, but then, once you can say it quickly, slow down! It's not a race!

Prepare yourself doubly for **stage fright** by assuming that the moment that you realize that dozens of other people are watching you, you'll probably forget about 40% of what you prepared, so it's best to over-prepare. Rehearse your material over and over again until everything flows easily and seems intuitive.

Lead. Sure, you practice hard to learn the material, but ultimately, there are aspects of prayer leading that cannot be learned in isolation; they have to be road tested. After your first time at the *amud*, you may well find that a number of issues you had been wrestling with previously will resolve themselves, and at the same time you'll realize that you need to work harder in some areas you thought you knew.

Here are some tips:

- Position one or two people on your right side who know the davenning, and ask them to help you through the process. Invite other people to sing with you [31] and to stand with you, so that you don't have to feel so lonely and exposed.

- Don't emphasize the overly tricky words – the ones, on which, in practice, you always seem to flub. Say the difficult words more quietly, until you're very confident with them.

- If you forget the *nusach* on the spot, just read the words, sing the same note as a monotone (single note) until you can remember the *nusach*, or simply ask somebody nearby (as long as it's not during certain prayers) to help you get it back in your head. Oftentimes, just saying the words out loud will be the best recourse. It's understandable that you might need a kickstart now and then; just do your best to get the ball rolling, and don't make a fuss.

- Confidence! Most people do not hear your mistakes, or even know the difference, so always present a calm, in-control demeanor, even if you feel you are messing up a lot. Somebody who looks in control can get away with a lot of mistakes, whereas somebody who looks nervous can lead a nearly perfect service and people will still think it wasn't right. FAKE it, with style! [32] Things will improve over time. Remember, everybody else is just an uncomfortable as you are. They want you to be confident, so they can be led and not have to worry about you, and rather focus on their own prayers.

- Smile, at least sometimes. Create a sense of joy throughout the process. I just can't say this enough.

The Artistry of the *Ba'al Tfilah:* 9
Leading, Listening, Responding, Creating

Once you've learned all of the correct *nusach* and have led davenning a few times, you'll be ready to work on the more advanced concepts that together constitute the artform of being a *ba'al tfilah*.

Consider all of the things a *ba'al tfilah* is trying to do at once: bringing together music, movement, language, leadership, listening. It's an artform, and a huge responsibility. Have patience! It takes many years to learn the music, to learn the words, to learn how to lead people with sensitivity, to learn to sense what's happening in a room and respond to it in kind. You could spend a lifetime, let alone a few decades, on such learning! In addition to having patience, both with yourself and your community, at the outset of integrating all these efforts, you might also want to keep some of the following concepts in mind. A number of them I've introduced to you previously. I restate them here because knowing what I'm shooting for, and being aware of the main points my audience is expecting of me, have been very helpful for me and I think they'll help you too.

Creating a reverent, intentional atmosphere

As a *ba'al tfilah*, one of your main jobs is to set up an atmosphere in the room that helps others to pray. Sound hard to define? It is, and yet there are definitely ways in which you can assess how well this devotional atmosphere is taking hold, and, if necessary, to encourage it to grow. My approach is to break "atmosphere" down into two levels, namely 1) There is the **underlying tone** that pervades the entire service, and 2) There are the **changing moods** that you cultivate throughout the service. The underlying tone that you set in the room, right from the beginning, should be one of *focus* and *intention* – in short, a sense of Occasion with a capital "O" that clearly communicates: "We're here on purpose. We did not stumble in here by accident. We *mean* to be doing this!" We call this intentionality *kavanah* (sacred intentionality).

Now, as I say, in addition to this underlying atmosphere of focused *kavanah*, there roam the ever-changing aesthetics and moods of the service – moods that range from somber to exultant. Your job as leader isn't just to surf these moods, it's also to model them, embody them, for the *kahal* (community). If a moment is quiet, you'll have to communicate "quietness." If a moment is regal, you'll have to communicate "regality." If a moment is serious, you'll have to communicate "solemnity." And if a moment is joyous, you'll have to come out of yourself a little bit and *lead* the joy in the room. The point is, that you're responsible for leading the aesthetic **and** emotional quality of the room. And yes, at the same time you must always bear in mind not to lose or distract from that underlying sense of overall focus and seriousness you've worked equally hard to achieve.

Encouraging aesthetic contrast and balance

As prayer leaders, we should count ourselves lucky: Jewish liturgical services have a lot of aesthetic ups and downs built into them, ranging from silence to exclamation, slow to fast, personal to communal, mundane to ecstatic. Aesthetic opposites are wonderful facilitators of communal prayer: they shed light on each other by means of contrast, and help to bring out different emotions and spiritual levels. As *ba'al tfilah*, it's your job to lead these ups and downs (much like a conductor of a symphony), so that people can experience the davenning-ride in a powerful way. Here are a few aesthetic considerations. I phrase them in the form of questions, things you might well ask yourself, while, and before, leading:

▪ **Pacing** How fast or slow should you go? Sometimes you'll need to race through pages and pages of text in just a few minutes. Other times, you may want to take ten minutes to sing one short paragraph. Most of the time, you'll settle into a moderate pace. It's up to you to decide how much time to spend on any given prayer, song, *nign*, or moment of silence. The basic idea is that you want to create a relaxed pace in which there is time for singing and beauty, but yet you also have to finish in time for people to go to lunch, and keep it moving fast enough that people don't feel like it drags. A good *ba'al tfilah* can *daven* very quickly, or stretch out moments to emphasize them; for this prayer leader the service becomes like a rubber band, sometimes stretching, and other times contracting, but always with a mind to maximize the spiritual power of the moment.

▪ **Dynamics** How loud or quiet should this moment be? In the realm of dynamics, you'll have to continuously decide just that, so get comfortable with...change. Your volume will range from silent to whispering, to normal to...power exclamation. Aside from the moments where one must be quiet (i.e., the silent *Amidah*), it's really up to you to decide! Consider the *Sh'ma*: Do you want to shout it out, so that all can "hear"?; Or, do you want to work from a quiet place, saying it sensitively, as if to say: "listen to the subtle sound of One-ness." Either way can be powerful, and what's more, you may take a different path each time you lead. All are valid. The important thing is to actively choose your path with that atmosphere we discussed earlier: to be aware.

▪ **Intensity** How much emotional energy and drama can you or should you pack into your service? Certainly, there are moments that deserve complete focus and outright emotional intensity. But these must be balanced against other moments that seem less intense, or else the intensity becomes overwhelming, if not off-putting.

▪ **Complexity** How artistically complex or simple is the music you are singing at any given point? Sometimes *ba'alei tfilah*, especially cantors, will want to sing a piece of music that's

B'fi Y'sharim (Simple Nusach)

B'fi Y'sharim (Elaborate Nusach)

As sung by Noach Schall
in traditional Ashkanazic Nusach

special, whose art helps bring meaning and beauty to the davenning. If you can do this, that's wonderful. But to have greatest impact, artistically complex moments such as these should be balanced by other extended areas of simple, humble davenning with no showiness.

▪ **Participation** How many people do you want singing right now? Sometimes you want the entire room to sing along. Other times you specifically want to create a quiet space in which you can sing the parts that are specifically designated for you as *shaliach tzibur*. Maybe you just want a gentle harmonic chord sung underneath you for color – and nothing else? That's fine. The service should not be "everybody all the time," or it will become static. [33] Pick good places for everybody to come in, and, conversely, for them to stay away. That way, you'll cultivate diversity, which is a good thing. All these different sounds will eventually emerge to form dramatic moments, throughout.

Giving clear cues and creating a transparency of intention

In order to facilitate the above-mentioned aesthetic contrasts, you're going to have to give very clear cues that are very easy to follow, ones that tell the *kahal* exactly what you are intending.

▪ **Cuing a congregational response** Scan your prayer ahead of time with the congregation in mind, as well as yourself. Locate all the points that occur right **before** the congregation is supposed to join in for an "out-loud" response and underline them in your book. When it's time for you to lead, and you're singing alone, and one of those parts comes up, punch it a bit so as to give the congregation a cue that they are about to join in. In short: pump up the volume in a few, key places of your own, and the *kahal* will remember to do their part, too. The first few times you try this, you might even want to leave a dramatic silence that says, "your turn!" This'll wake them up so that they respond with the appropriate "Amen" or other response. If you're supposed to say a particular word or phrase with them in a prayer, then say it loud and proud. If you're not supposed to say it, then make sure that you stay out of their way, so they can do it themselves. Sometimes a deafening silence from you is just what's needed to perk people up.

- **Starting, continuing, and ending melodies** Start a melody with a clear first few notes; later, when it's about to finish, communicate to those around you with a nod or a hand gesture – or simply by slowing down – that on your cue, the melody is about to end. If you're going to continue the melody (merging it into another round of a wordless *nign*, for instance) prepare people at the end of the vocalized section, making it clear that "this isn't over yet!" When you're transitioning from one musical phrase to another, prepare people with "guide tones" or with "ay yai yai"-type vocalizations that forecast the note that's coming up. Remember: transparent intentions allow others to participate less hesitantly. Always strive to be 100% clear about what **you're** going to do. Your reward will be a confident and more enthusiastic *kahal*.

- **Establishing clear tempo** Establish a beat and stay with it. Don't indulge in haphazard rhythm. Keep the beat either auditorally, with a confident (but sensitive) percussive pound on the *shtender* [34] or visually, by conducting the *kahal* with clear movements of your hand or body, so that it's absolutely clear what rhythm you are intending. Often, your body can communicate rhythm quite well. Even when your feet have to stay together in one place, as in the *Amidah*, you can bounce up and down gently on your toes. Try this especially when your back is to the *kahal* – a time when whatever service you're leading is most susceptible to rhythm loss. Of course, you may need to work on rhythm yourself in order to be an effective, human tempo-keeper! [35]

- **Managing intensity** If you want the room to pick up steam, you'll have to urge that process along by clearly increasing your own output of energy, making it clear with your body language that you want the energy to increase in the room as a whole. However, try to do this as a slow surge, rather than a sudden shift, wherever possible. You never want to appear to be pushing too hard, or it will seem that you are detached from the *kahal*. Think: Slow and steady rises. For example, if you want to get the energy up for "L'cha Dodi," start slowly increasing the energy one and a half psalms earlier, so that by the time "L'cha Dodi" comes around, the energy is already up in the room.

- **Maintaining focus** If the room gets too noisy (with lots of people talking, kids rustling, or other distracting sounds), you may have to reestablish control of the room with a respectful cue. Pause, hold still, and wait for people to hear their own noise, and they'll get the message without your having to resort to more commandeering gestures (which probably won't be of much use, anyway). This is the most respectful way of re-asserting communal focus, but use it only sparingly. You can't have control all the time, so pick your battles and go for only the important moments.

- **Directing your energy**
Sometimes you can make your intentions obvious by simply modeling with your own body what you'd like others to do. Consider where you are directing your energy. If you're focusing downward toward your *siddur*, your posture suggests an inward, introspective moment of personal reflection. If you

Where the leader's energy is directed shows different aspects of prayer...

face upwards, a reaching up toward the heavens is more or less implied. If you are directing your energy outward around the room, it suggests connection with the community of daveners, as if to say, "We're doing this together! Let's go!" There are appropriate moments for all of these energies, so use them to good advantage.

Overall, be prepared. While trying to give clear cues of any kind, the most important thing for you do it is *think ahead*, so that you're ready to give the cues when they come along. Lead decisively. There are often multiple ways to do any particular part of the service, but ONE of them needs to happen, and it's your job to make that happen. Your job is to decide for the *kahal* what you feel the best course is to take, and then ACT on it. Getting the jump on the situation will allow the people around you feel a sense of ownership of their own ability to follow, to draw together more competently and confidently in prayer.

Choosing Melodies for a Service:

As a prayer leader, you select melodies for people to sing together. You decide how many melodies to sing (and also when NOT to sing), and which melody to use for any parcel of text. At a very advanced level, some *ba'alei tfilah* choose melodies on the spot, and even set a text to different melodies that happen to pop into their heads. But at first, you'll want to carefully plan out your melody routes, to make sure you've got some strong material that will help the *kahal* sing together.

First, make sure you know all the melodies that are commonly sung where you are davenning. Many of them will be really good, so sing them! When you use the melodies that people know, that are already in place, you'll be more likely to get some response. But sometimes, understandably, you'll want to introduce a new melody, because you really don't like one of the established melodies, or because you feel that the congregation needs the energy that a new melody can bring.

If so, your best bet for success is to try to introduce the new melodies outside of the service. Teach a group of friends ahead of time, so that you have some people who are guaranteed to know the melodies when you start. You want a new melody to succeed the first time, so that it gets the right communal energy and people want to do it again next time. The same new melody can be overwhelmingly wonderful, or it can flop, all depending upon how well you prepare people for it. Teach ahead of time!

There are some great singing shuls that can have gotten to the stage where they are listening well enough to each other that they can pick up new melodies on the fly. If you know that your *kahal* is with you and would be happy to learn a new melody, then sometimes you can introduce new melodies while a service is happening. Even so, do that only occasionally, so that the majority of any service remains familiar to people. Rather than trying to sing all your favorite melodies in one service, right away, take the long view, and introduce one or two at a time. Over several years, people will really come to know and love them. Innovate too quickly, however, and people will loose focus, fast. It just takes too much concentration to learn more that one or two melodies in a few hours.

Now that I've told you to be cautious, to look, as it were, at both sides of the (new) coin, there is a bonus to forging ahead, and it's a big one: introducing melodies into a *kahal* is one of the most satisfying experiences a *ba'al tfilah* can have. **What makes a melody appropriate in a given section of liturgy?** And how will you know it's really working? Here are a few concepts for you to consider:

1. **Word-Fit:** Does the melody fit the words? The melody must physically "fit" with the words, e.g., you must be able to sing the words without having to scrunch too many words in a last-second scramble at the end of a long sentence. (Sound familiar?) Some sets of words, like "Yigdal," and "El Adon," are set up metrically so that they can work with just about any melody that comes along. Others are far less obvious, and require some careful planning. Go over the words carefully ahead of time, to make sure they marry well with the melody. In addition, try to sing the words in the same way that they are commonly phrased in different (and more familiar) settings, to make the word-breaks as predictable for people as possible. For example, if you're setting "Mimkomcha" to a new melody, and you need to repeat a word to fit the text to the melody, [36] you might consider repeating the words *"L'dor Va'dor"* because in many other melodies those same two words repeat. The more people can logically expect, and anticipate, what might need to happen, the more likely it is that your new melody will succeed.

2. **Tonality:** How does the tonality relate to the *nusach*? Is the melody in Major, Minor, or *Freygish*? And, what's more, how does that relate to the *nusach* of the particular part of service you're in? Here there are no set rules, namely, you're not required to sing a melody in the same tonality as the surrounding *nusach*, but if you do, you might find that it comes off as a better fit. Overall, working "together" with the *nusach*, rather than competing with it, is a good thing. Consider the following melody. "Yakar Nign" that's used as a *nign* after the 2nd psalm in *Kabalat Shabbat* at Yakar in Jerusalem. It's in major, so it works very well with the major *nusach* of *Kabalat Shabbat*. Or, consider the following traditional melody for "Or Chadash" for *Shabbat Shacharit*. It works tonally because it is in *Freygish*, and the *nusach* surrounding it is also in *Freygish*, so the two support each other. To be sure, though, it's okay

Yakar Nign

To be sung between 2nd and 3rd Psalms Kabbalat Shabbat

Or Chadash

to put in a melody in a tonality that contradicts the *nusach*, as long as the melody still seems to work for other reasons.

3. **Mood:** What is the mood of the melody? Does the mood reflect the mood of the prayer? How does the mood of the melody fit into the mood of the prayer service as a whole? If you are trying to pick up the energy of the room after a long bunch of solo *nusach* moments, then use a faster melody. If you are trying to create a sense of deep yearning, you may use a slower, 3/4 melody. However, identifying a melody as "happy," or "sad" or "uplifting," or "longing" is highly subjective. Is a fast melody joyous, a slow melody mournful? For example, some people claim that "Yism'chu" (in the *Shabbat Musaf* service) which focuses largely on the joyousness of *Shabbat*, should be fast – to demonstrate immediate, energetic joy. Others take the same text and insist that "Oneg" refers to a "spiritual joy," and that a slower melody leaves more room for this *shabbosdik*, spiritual joy.

Yism'chu

M'nucha V'Simcha

As sung by Asher Schmerler

Similarly, research a melody for the *zemer* "M'nucha v'simcha": you'll be sure to find fast versions, slow versions, and medium versions, the latter of which presumably tries to draw a balance between *m'nucha* (rest) and *simcha* (joyousness). All of these can be said to 'fit.' Choose well, and with a purpose to create and fit the mood you're after, and you'll do fine.

Ultimately, one person's joy may be another's sorrow. One person's tonal conflict is a dissonance lover's delight! While there are some extremes that are objectively wrong, melody selection and application is often quite subjective. There are few clear-cut answers, except to look at the room and decide if people are singing and engaging. This lack of absolute answers leaves room for the individual artistry of the *ba'al tfilah*.

Picking a Key:

If you're trying to lead a *kahal* in singing, you're going to want to pick a key that the majority of people can sing comfortably in. If you're lucky, your normal voice range coincides with the comfort range of the majority. If you're not in that range, you'll have some choices to make.

Consider the range of the melody. Is it a small range (i.e. it never seems very low or very high)? Then you don't have to think too hard, because most people will be able to manage no matter where you start. But if it's a large range, then you have to be careful. If a melody gets very high in the second section, you should start as low as possible, if even just for you to make it through the high part that's coming.

Sure enough, the first step is finding a key that you can comfortably sing in. But keys get more complex when you imagine trying to optimize the singing situation for all present, Hence, you'll eventually be confronted with the choice as leader whether to do what's comfortable for you, or to do what you think will work best for everyone. By the way, you'll never make everyone happy all the time (there's just to much of a range of voices out there!), so take heart.

The general names for singing ranges are bass (lowest), tenor, alto, soprano (highest). Say, for example, you're a guy with not the highest, but not the lowest voice, like myself. you're probably a tenor. If you start a melody in a comfortable place for you, the soprano women will be able to sing along, comfortably, but the altos will get caught in the middle. Sing lower, and the sopranos will be too low. Somebody is always left out of melody range, so let's just hope they can sing harmonies, and move along. If you listen to others while leading, after a while you'll start to realize who is singing along comfortably, and who has to awkwardly skip into different octaves in order to finish the melody.

What's important is that you get to know *how your voice range compares to others,* and, subsequently, learn how to ascertain when it's the right time to purposefully (and compassionately) sing in your not-so-ideal key for the sake of the greater good. When singing melodies with everyone, try to pick the key that works for the majority. If, however, you're singing a solo piece with other people merely doing "Ah's" or "Amens," or chanting the *nusach,* et al, it's better to choose the range that's perfect for you, so that you can be heard clearly and beautifully.

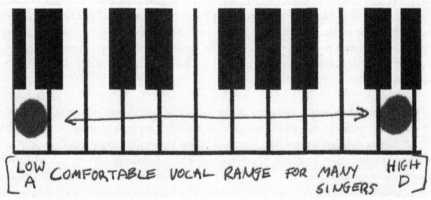

So how do you find the right key? Lead a number of times and keep your ears open. You'll think, "Next time I do that melody I better start a little lower (or higher)." Unless you have a band with you that helps you sing a good key (which never happens in many shuls), you'll have to just practice finding that spot that works with people, and you can only do that by singing with people until you start to intuitively understand the various "sweet spots" for singing. [37]

Charismatic Leadership and "Getting Out of the Way"

The tricky part about being a prayer leader is that it's your job both to lead powerfully, and at the same time to stay out of the way, so that others can have their own experience of prayer. Thus, you can't get too emotional, or too artistic, etc., or people will be distracted from their own davenning. And yet you can't stay entirely out of the way, or you may have missed an opportunity to lead a community into something greater than the sum of its parts. What to do?

Charismatic leadership can be useful if funneled into the right purposes. In order for people to come together to create anything meaningful or artistic, there is nothing like a point person egging them on, reminding them why they're here, and what they're trying to do (think: soccer captain, musical conductor...you name it). If this person seems believable, compelling, flexible and wise, in other words, has charisma, people are more likely to perk up and follow.

Some people have a natural showmanship, a natural charisma, and it's easy for them to attract attention. These types of leaders must always temper their charisma into serving the community. Ask yourself: "Is this about me, or is this about helping the community to develop?" These are difficult issues of menschlikhkeit that must be worked on internally by any capable leader.

Many people, however, have the opposite problem: they feel they couldn't summon up a good performance if their lives depended upon it. They need to develop their confidence, style, and courage, so that they can get up there and make something happen. They must work on presenting a confident, compelling leadership style.

No matter what kind of leader you are, you must curtail your leadership whenever possible, to open up space for people to lead themselves. The *Shulchan Aruch* [38] (Code of Jewish Law) says that a *shaliach tzibur* may sing beautifully, but it cannot be "just to hear his own voice." This is the endless balance between the need for passionate – even daring – leadership and at the same time to ultimately externalize some of the concepts of humility that you may even be reciting aloud (especially on the high holidays)-like "Mei'afar...Le'afar"("from dust to dust.")

"Getting out of the way" applies musically, also. How loud should you sing? You should balance strong, outright, forceful singing (when it's called for to lead the room) with very delicate singing that lets others take over. Sometimes you really have to lead strongly and confidently; other times you have to get out of the way. Amazingly, sometimes when you remove your own loud voice from the mix, you realize that you were pushing too hard, and that *it's actually happening beautifully on its own.* Let it happen on its own, and take a break. As a leader, you must continually demonstrate both how to lead and how to listen. Ask yourself "Am I listening?............ space space space...... Am I hearing everybody else?...............?" Do the minimum amount of loud singing that you can get away with.

Try to notice people's funny quirks and particulars, and wink at them when they do it. Elise always sings that particular harmony. Robbie always does a specific finger roll in the debka rhythm. Josh always declares "L'taken Olam B'malchut Shadai" out loud during Aleinu. Those quirks are the specialness of a community. Take them as little cues, if you will; see them with compassion, and you'll find they'll provide you lots of opportunities to connect with people. Finally, as often as possible, let someone else lead, and step to the side to actively demonstrate how to follow. Stand next to the other leader; sing, rock, and give them the same sensitive responsiveness you'd want if you were leading yourself. Teach others to imitate you as you follow. **Often, you make more progress towards getting people to sing when you're not the singing leader – but when you're the follower!**

Becoming Part of the Tradition

Before you start getting creative with the music or service, make sure that you've studied the existing tradition as much as possible, and that it becomes a fixed study throughout your life. The more you lead, the more you are becoming part of the historical tradition of leading services that dates back thousands of years. While any historical study would be beyond the limits of this book, consider learning about the following historical Jewish-musical traditions: the *Taamim* (tropes) of the Torah, the chants of the Levite *meshor'rim* (choristers), the orchestras that played in the Temple, the songs of Moshe and Miriam, the songs of David, the Misinai melodies identified by the Maharil in the 15th century, the Baal Shem Tov's *nigunim* (18th c.), the thousands of melodies for *zmirot* and prayer texts, the great traditions of *chazzonic* artistry, the intricate *nuschaot* that prayer are sung with, the great Jewish instrumental traditions that flourished despite instrumental bans, the dozens of different folk-song traditions (Yiddish and Ladino songs, for example), the tremendous contributions of Jews to other music traditions around the world, and the ongoing development of new songs, music, and cultural traditions.

Being aware of the rich liturgical history of davenning past will imbue your present davenning with a sense of continuity and tradition, and, as such, will serve to deepen your leadership ability. As *shaliach tzibur*, you're responsible for upholding the tradition, but at the same time, you become the intermediary in the present between the past and the future. Prayer has changed a lot in our history, but was always deeply informed by what came before it. If we are deeply informed, then our creativity will become part of the chain of development of the tradition, a living tradition, that takes us in new directions all the time.

PART IV:

BUILDING SINGING COMMUNITIES

Dveykus Nign

Joey Weisenberg

Chaim's Waltz

Joey Weisenberg

Politics and Diplomacy 10

Building a singing core, developing a good architectural space, teaching melodies, learning the art of the *ba'al tfilah* – these are all the things we need to do in order to create a singing community. In some lucky communities, the majority of people quickly take to these ideas, and you can work directly to use the strategies in this book. But in many communities, sometimes it's hard to accomplish even the beginning of any of these strategies, because there is so much politics, inertia, and just plain baffling resistance standing in the way. In these communities you often have to work *indirectly*, taking a long-term approach that you hope will create a singing community three to ten years down the line. Have patience, and enjoy the process!

The Arguments *Against* Singing: Hear them first, then gear up your coping mechanisms. No one said change was easy.

Beyond a doubt, you will encounter lots of resistance to the idea of singing in the shul, and much of the time, **you should listen carefully,** as we all have something to learn from each other about different prayer styles. Simply put, **"intimate singing"** is not for everyone. Some prefer an open, quiet, and relatively private prayer experience; sitting in their *makom* (particular seat) in the shul, where they can have space for quiet, meaningful, and, most important here, personal time. Understandably, these are the folks who might likewise suggest that it would be most prudent to value the sacred silence they've worked so hard to cultivate in their davenning and on *Shabbat* above all else, and that you do the same. Some feel that lots of singing distracts from the words of the prayers, which they believe are primary. Others feel that synagogue music should remain the purview of *chazzan* or *ba'al tfilah* and choir, where, they feel, the music can reach greater artistic and spiritual heights. Some love to sing, but want to emphasize singing in other places, such as the *Shabbat* table, instead of in the service itself. I would count these to be among the most important objections to singing you'll encounter. Of course, they should be sincerely addressed and carefully considered in striking the best **singing-silence balance** for your shul.

At the same time, there exist other types of resistance that are much more frustrating to deal with, largely because they don't represent a deeply felt objection to some aspect of communal singing. Rather, they are simply discouraging, seemingly immovable obstacles, passively maintained by years and years of stagnant communal inertia. For example, say the aspiring *ba'al tfilah* wants to lead services one week from the middle of the room, rather than the *bimah*. [39] An innocent enough idea? But let's imagine what sorts of responses he or she might receive in a shul where this has rarely, if ever, been done before. These are responses of the this-is-an-insurmountable-problem variety that I'm talking about:

"Oh no! We can't do that; I'm used to walking down the center aisle, not the side!"
"It's not in the synagogue's by-laws – we'll have to call a ritual committee special session."
"I mean, it just wouldn't be safe – a fire code violation for sure."
"That's really a decision for the board to make. We'll try to get it on the agenda for the next meeting three months from now."
"No, that couldn't work, the microphone cord doesn't stretch that far."

And everybody's favorite,
"Why would we do that? I've never seen that before."

The list goes on and on of things some congregants and shuls will do to avoid accommodating even the easiest ideas. This lack of willingness to even consider simple new ideas amounts to a sort of passive sabotage that many shuls inflict on any promising innovation. That said, it can be overcome!

For those who want to create a singing community, there are basically two routes, both of which follow the same patterns as any process of communal change. One is to work from within an existing synagogue and take the long-term (and sometimes frustrating) approach toward change, slowly pressuring from within and patiently waiting for people to understand and encourage your vision. The other approach is to start a new *minyan* from scratch, which gives you lots of freedom but leaves you resource-poor and in need of recreating many of the communal structures that already existed elsewhere. In the last decade, we've witnessed the explosion of independent *minyanim* around the country who understandably opt to start their own prayer groups rather than endure the frustrations of dealing with the established synagogues. But before you flee and start your own group, take some time to assess your existing community shuls, as there is a lot of potential for change and growth within them that might not strike you initially.

The following is a list of a few strategies that will help in building singing in your community. The goal is to create a "buy-in" from all corners of the community. In every community, you'll have to be a sales person to talk to people, to build trust, etc. In short, these are much the same qualities that you'd use to build a business. Henceforth, I encourage you to think of yourself as a kind of peace-vending, music-loving entrepreneur.

Get to know people! Cultivate relationships with people in the community, *one at a time.* Amazingly, one good relationship can lead to so much more good will down the line. That one person feels included, and then he or she invites another... Once you get the relationship ball rolling, it can expand dramatically.

Kiddush: Work it. This time-tested, built-in, social affair after services provides a great, low-stress opportunity to meet people and create energy around the idea of singing. You can generate more genuine enthusiasm by talking one-on-one with six different people at a short kiddish than you can in hours of impersonal back-and-forths via e-mail and phone. However, a word of caution before you run around the shul community room, determined to reach out to

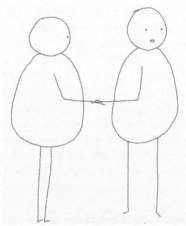
Looking over the shoulder

each and every congregant: don't be an "Over-The-Shoulder-Looker", don't look around for someone who's ostensibly more important to talk to than the one you're talking to right now. Stay focused. It just isn't necessary to be so *macher*-driven. Everybody has a meaningful place and role in the community and contributes in his or her own way. Sometimes the person you'd overlook at first turns out to be the cornerstone of your effort later on.

Cultivate an outgoing attitude. Winks, eye contact, firm handshakes and other tools of basic human interaction help people feel at home. So greet everybody. Make a habit of shaking every person's hand, and even getting up (as in, out of your seat) [40] to do it in a friendly way. You don't have to become a big phony/small-talk type, but you do have to go out of your way to create positive energy in the room.

Remember people's names. Remember names and details of people, without regard to who is "important". Remembering names is very difficult for most of us, but try your best. Make a photo book of members or students. Look at the shul walls for donors, pore over membership lists, prepare yourself, so when you meet someone, you'll have at least heard of their name before. When you can identify somebody warmly, by name, you instantly create a sense of confidence in a relationship. As a model of this, I think of Rebbetzin Feige Twerski in Milwaukee, Wisconsin, who is particularly gifted at remembering everybody she ever met.

Consult with the "Old-Timers." Set up meetings with congregants who have been around for much longer than yourself. Ask questions like, "What are your favorite *nusach* melodies?" or, "How do you envision the musical future of this Shul?" These meetings of consultation show that you're open to all ideas and are not only out there trying to push your own agenda. The process of meeting with established members of the shul creates feelings of trust and understanding that help everybody move forward.

Invite people personally. Invite people to events individually. If you want to get ten people to stand with you for the first attempt at a "Singing Core," then ask each person directly to come and sing with you. The personal touch is vastly more effective, not to mention more in the character of the engagement we're after anyway, than sending a mass e-mail or putting up a flier (though those are essential, too). Eventually, once you know people, you can move on and meet new people, and invite those new people individually, and then your participation will blossom. However, (especially at first), it's one person at a time!

Bring in "ringers." When you're getting started, bring in friends who know how to sing the melodies you know. They serve as lighter fluid, helping to create a starter flame while the larger log decides if it will take. If something succeeds at the beginning, people will get the idea faster, and start participating, and then before long you won't need the ringers anymore (but all the better if they stay!).

Resuscitate an unattended service: Sometimes, it's better to start your singing-community efforts outside of the "prime-time" of *Shabbat* morning. For example, Kabbalat *Shabbat* often has very low attendance, but has amazing musical potential, is a very flexible service overall, and has lots of musical opportunities and existing traditions to draw from. This is a great place to start a singing service, because change there is likely to be met with less resistance. Few people are as invested in it as they are in, say, *Shabbat Musaf*. If you succeed with Kabbalat *Shabbat*, people may begin to ask, "Why can't we sing like this in *all* of our services?"

Create Alternative Opportunities for Singing If you feel that there is not sufficient interest in making simple changes that will facilitate singing during davenning, don't push it. You don't want to force your vision of singing on other people. In these cases, consider encouraging group singing at other times of *Shabbat*. Sing around the table at meals. Create a *tisch* or *seudah shlishit* [41] where singing can happen free of any other liturgical interests. Or, you can make communal music in different spaces, as an alternative to services. For example, at my shul in Brooklyn, the rabbi and I decided it wouldn't be wise to move in and "force" changes on the main *Shabbat* morning service immediately, but rather to develop music in other parts of the shul, on the periphery, such as an alternative singing service that meets every other *Shabbat*. After three years of attending that service, a lot more people in the shul have experienced the possibility of communal singing, and are starting to request that we figure out how to do it in the main space. Pick your fights, and temper your singing vision so that it fits the place, and acknowledges the different people who are there.

Teach, teach, teach individuals. You must train lots of people in the community to help with the singing. Train them to lead the services themselves, and then they'll understand more about how to follow, too! One-on-one teaching is also an excellent way to build personal relationships that will keep growing over time.

Teach classes. Teach a class (or ten) that's open to the community, in which you discuss, for example, the history of synagogue music, or something along those lines. Bring in lots of old books; Jews love to look at books. I brought in a collection of 40 songbooks for one lecture, and I barely needed to speak at all. I considered it a guided tour through song-book history, and frequently quoted my grandmother, may her memory be a blessing, who as an art museum docent who used to stand in front of a painting asking, "Nu, what do you *see?*" Teach with the same do-it-ourselves-together philosophy that leads us to sing together, rather than telling people what to think top-down. Empower them to figure it out themselves by looking directly at primary documents.

Teach children, but keep equal focus on adults. Teach children and teenagers, and you'll reap two rewards: First, you'll train the future generation of leaders (and have fun doing it!), and second, you'll make important connections with their parents. That said, remember to teach adults, too, so that adults can model Jewish life for their children. An actively learning adult population encourages children to become learners in the long-term.

Communicate and keep everybody "in the loop." If you go out of your way to inform the right people about things, they will feel included, and help pave the way for more. For example, when using a shul building, even for a meeting with just one person, make sure to always consult with the building manager, even if you can't imagine there could be a problem. This keeps up a feeling amongst different people that they are on the same page. The feeling of open communication about even basic items can really help keep a group positive, whereas forgetting to communicate even a small, seemingly insignificant item could result in hurt feelings – and sometimes worse.

Pace the introduction of new ideas. Here's a case study: I call it Inconspicuous Clapping. If you go into a normal shul and start clapping excitedly all the time, people won't understand what you're doing. What's more, they'll think you're crazy and get annoyed. As an alternative, use the "knee slap," which is

Inconspicuous knee slap

essentially an "under the radar clap," as you can slap your knee inconspicuously and pretend it's not happening, and then it won't make some people uncomfortable. Pacing musical innovations makes people feel like music is just an organic thing, seeping in from outta nowhere. And that's a good thing.

Ask for feedback, and make changes whenever possible. Solicit feedback from everybody you talk to. This way people are a part of the action. If you listen to them and make positive changes and credit them with a good idea, then you've got a partnership! A congregant complained of too much banging, and so we started using a much more sensitive *shtender* percussion approach. The results ended up being much more musical. So it was win-win.

Stick to your guns sometimes. Of course, you'll have to accept negative feedback; just also know that it's OK to have some issues or instances on which you're not prepared to compromise. For example, a woman was complaining about the fact that we put the *shtender* in the aisle on *Shabbos* morning, and that she hated having to walk to her seat from the other side of the pew. I explained the importance of having the *shtender* in the center of the room, but she still wouldn't have it. So, we had to politely remain adamant; eventually the *shtender* in the middle aisle stayed.

To make even common-sense changes, you must be prepared to occasionally tick people off. All the more so when you make bigger changes, or implement certain strains of new ideas. *Shacharit*, for instance, despite its restful tone on *Shabbat,* can be a real tinderbox. When we started a separate, bi-monthly "singing session" on *Shabbat* morning (yes, during *Shacharit*, but in a separate room), some people were outraged and declared, "you're trying to divide the shul!" Two years later, some of those same people became regulars at our singing session, and have expressed sincere interest in carrying the same singing energy they experienced in our alternative space back into the main shul service.

Support everybody else, too. Just as you'd like to be supported, make sure to support others in their ventures. Go to classes that other people are teaching. Allow yourself to learn from others, and they'll be more interested in learning from you.

Thank people. Saying thank you to people may seem like common-sense manners, but when lots of things are going on, and the seasons rush forward, it can be easy to forget to thank people for their work, volunteering, singing, participation, etc. Ideally, you should write thank you letters after big events. But a simple e-mail or phone call can make for a good and welcome gesture when a formal letter is just too hard to pen.

Never assume it will work. Once I brought my favorite walking drum – a huge, attention-getting circular drum I play strapped to my chest with a deep, resonant 'boom' to a season opening event for Mechon Hadar (the educational institute in Manhattan that also consults to independent minyanim). Because the room was full of hundreds of young *Hadarniks,* (translation: a hip and energetic group, overall) I assumed that if I started playing the drum and singing a well-known *nign*, that people would eagerly respond with lots of singing. Instead, I started banging on the drum and singing while people stared I was feeling lonelier and lonelier by the minute as everyone went back to talking. Looking back on what went wrong, I realized that a quick word ahead of time might have been all that was needed to get the room singing – only I hadn't given it. Lesson: Always frame what's going to happen for the audience, by quickly [42] explaining with a short preface to get people on board.

Don't freeze. Keep creating. As our great sage Hillel tells us in Pirkei Avot, if you don't increase your knowledge of Torah, it will decrease. It's the same with creative musical ventures, including the communal. Unfortunately, there's never a point at which you can get comfortable and think, "we've arrived." The minute you start thinking like that, everything will go downhill! You need to keep producing new ideas and striving to make them happen. That's the only way to maintain the ideas you have already cultivated and fought for.

Smile when it does work: When it all works, smile and take pleasure, because tomorrow will present new challenges and it will be a struggle all over again.

Push forward, but have patience!!! A singing community can emerge quickly if you're starting out with a group of friends, but if you're working against decades of inertia, communal musical progress can take many years. Creating momentum in a community involves a subtle balance between urgently pushing forward, and patiently allowing things to unfold in their time. Prepare yourself for a journey, and onwards!

Expanding the Musical Culture of the Community 11

The community sings. **Now what?** If you feel that your community has arrived, and that it's now a true singing community, then have another look at it. Start over. Reboot. Re-examine your community's music: As we've said earlier, the process of musical creation is never over – it's simply a temporary, evanescent moment of time filled with music which vanishes the next day, and demands an entirely new effort. Musicians have a similar feeling after they've given a huge concert, or recorded a new album: "Wow, that was a lot of work, and it happened, and...Oh...now it's gone and in the past, and I've got to dream up something else..."

This is the perfect time to start refocusing on each other. Ask evaluatory questions, like, "Are we really listening to each other?" Or, "Is the davenning experience the same every week, or does it vary, and for what reasons, good or bad?" Refine the musical artistry of your shul. Rather than singing loud all the time, try to respond to one another, to vary tonalities, and rhythms, and even change up tunes spontaneously. Go ahead and introduce more melodies, but not because the other ones aren't good enough.

Beyond the singing-specific strategies that have occupied most of this book, here are some suggestions for added activities that will not only create a sense of variety within the Group Singing Experience (variety being the 'spice' of all aesthetic life), but will also, in the long run, shore up the foundations of what you've already built.

Create community bands.

Community bands, such as *klezmer* bands or Jewish music ensembles, offer alternative musical/spiritual experiences to amateur musicians. The bands can also play at *havdallahs*, *melave malkas*, Purim, and other communal *simchas*. In the same way that we create informal Jewish choirs, when musicians get together to make Jewish music, the life of the shul is greatly enhanced.

In general, even if they're not in a formal band, encourage musicians to play in your synagogue as often as possible. Instrumental music is just like singing a *nign*; it's pure melody, simple, beautiful, and unencumbered by text. Playing Jewish music (or any music) on one's instrument can be a deeply spiritual experience, one which can be felt by the performer as deeply and as keenly as any prayer experience.

Furthermore, the secular nature of *klezmer* music is actually helpful for some people, who may seek alternate outlets for their Jewish energy. If you can bring secular and religious Jewish music together in your communities, you're on your way to restoring the symbiotic relationship that used to exist between the secular and religious in our Jewish world. The study of instrumental history should inform and support the study of *nigunim* and liturgical music.

Create a band, and hire a Jewish music coach for the band; and what better teacher than an experienced, local, *klezmer* musician? There are a number of amazing klezmer musicians out there who can help amateurs learn the instrumental traditions and play beautifully. Overall, having a coach is essential for the same reasons that having a *nusach* teacher is essential: there's only so much sense you can make of a musical tradition on your own, without input from a practitioner. Let's not forget that Jewish music is a living tradition, after all.

Create MP3's for the community.

One ongoing project is to record MP3's for people to use as learning tools. People can put the MP3's on their iPod and listen to the music during the week – effectively getting the melodies into their ears so they're ready to sing them out when *Shabbos* comes around.

Write a community songbook.

Another way to really bring out the musicality of a community is to work together to create a community songbook. Interview members of various ages, capture the best melodies, transcribe them, and print them in a book that can be read anytime. We've been creating such a song book at the Kane Street shul in Brooklyn, and a lot of people have gotten involved in the project. We've decided to focus on what was unique about our community's music, rather than trying to include every single song we sing. By focusing on the unique, we encourage local musical cultures and creativity, rather than trying to achieve one overarching, unified and, ultimately, very limited Jewish musical world.

Write new music.

Write new *nigunim*, settings for liturgical music, and choral pieces, and use them in your community when it makes sense. This way, you can begin to re-create vibrant local musical traditions, ones which imbue your worship-community with a specific musical personality.

Create a concert series.

For local Jewish music, and bring in international performers when feasible. Hosting a concert in your shul is a great way to support local and international Jewish culture. Support local first, as it's much more economical, builds good will, and continues to give back locally over time (because the musicians don't leave town the day after the gig). But if there's money left over, it would be great to have touring artists come in and play music that you don't get to hear every day. When I heard Andy Statman play in my Milwaukee shul when I was 16 years old, his mastery made a lasting impression on me and gave me something to aspire to.

Start up a Jewish dance circle.

Reconnect the body with music. Some people love to move, and dance groups facilitate this. Also, once you have a few good dancers in the community, it becomes a lot more fun when a communal *simcha* happens. Strike up the *kapelye* (ensemble) and you've got a few ringleaders who know some steps and are not embarrassed. To facilitate learning dance, bring in teachers who know some of the old Jewish dance traditions, but don't be afraid to make up your own!

Play instruments during services.

Throughout the course of this book, I've avoided the topic of using instruments during services because traditionally, and in many parts of the Jewish world currently, instruments are forbidden on *Shabbat*. Of course, vast numbers of shuls regularly use instruments to great spiritual effect, including guitars, percussion, organs, and full bands and even miniature orchestras. My personal feeling is that voices alone are enough to create a wonderful, *shabbosdik* musical atmosphere, especially when you take the time to get set up the way we've discussed earlier. However, I've got mixed feelings on this, as I've got lots of friends who play instruments during services and, with them, create lots of beauty every week for their *kahal*. As a compromise, any shul across the observance spectrum could consider using instruments until the end of L'cha Dodi, before *Ma'ariv* starts. This has several precedents in Jewish history. It is said that the Mitler Rebbe of Lubavitch had a *kapelye* which played until *Maariv* as a warm-up to *Shabbos*. However, suffice it to say that if you are using instruments during davenning, all the ideas in this book still apply. You'd still want to locate the *ba'al tfilah* in the center of the room, away from a raised, proscenium stage, surrounded by musicians as well as musical *gabbaim* in a tight musical core that now simply includes...instruments! This new, instrument-inclusive core then leads the room in davenning.

I wrote this book to help foster a more musical Jewish world - but as explained in the book, it's not only about singing. It's about coming closer together to hear each other. It's about listening and paying attention. It's about teaching and learning, building and creating. It's about allowing musical and spiritual beauty to transcend the limits of the individual. I hope that the practical strategies offered in this book can inspire and empower a few more people to go out there and re-create communities both musical and holy, in the best senses of the terms. Thank you for reading, and I'll look forward to singing with you down the line!

ACKNOWLEDGEMENTS

While I take responsibility for any deficiencies in this book, so many of the successful concepts that follow are merely ideas that I've picked up along the way from my teachers, friends, students, musical heroes, and family. Thank you so much to some of my teachers over the years who generously introduced me to the ever-expanding path of musicality: Bill Stone, Doug Owens, Mike Rupsch, Barry Mitterhoff, Howard Alden, Andy Statman and to those who helped me specifically in Jewish music: Cantor Carey Cohen, Rabbi Michel Twerski, Cantor Noach Schall and many others. Jeff Warschauer, in particular, mentored me to become a musician, empowered me to become a teacher of klezmer music (at Klez Kanada), and most recently suggested that I write what became this book.

Thank you to Rabbi Elie Kaunfer, who gave me a start as a teacher of Jewish singing. Seven years later, and I'm teaching at the Yeshiva he co-founded and writing a book that he's publishing.

Thank you to the team that has made this book a reality – Julie Meslin for her adorable potato-people illustrations, Sarah Schmerler for her careful editing work and coaching me through the process of writing, Nancy Ettenheim for her time-intensive proofreading work, and Ginny Prince for her careful layout and beautiful graphic design work.

Thank you to so many friends who have taught me melodies and cared enough to sing for long periods of time; Eric Gold, Lani Santo, Robbie Dvorkin, Elise Bernhardt, Chaim Kranzler, and so many others.

Thank you to Kane Street Shul, and everybody there who has created a beautiful singing community and nurtured me as I've put some of the ideas in this book to consistent use. Rabbi Sam Weintraub and Rabbi Simkha Weintraub have been especially helpful in encouraging all of these musical endeavors.

Thank you to all of my students and teachers at Yeshivat Hadar and in synagogues around the country who have created so many wonderful moments together with me, and who have helped me to understand the dynamics of singing groups.

Thank you to my parents Nancy Ettenheim and Bob Weisenberg who demonstrated and taught me about the wonders of harmony and rhythm from an early age, and who have always encouraged me to dream. Thank you to my brother Sam who has sung with me through many of these experiments, and to the rest of my immediate and extended families who have helped me to come to the sorts of life-realizations that have distilled themselves into the musical ideas I've presented here.

Finally, thank you to my wife, Molly Weingrod, who has strongly supported this project and many others, and whose suggestions have contributed to this book directly, and with whom I've been privileged to live and sing.

FOOTNOTES

1. Kalib, Sholom, The Musical Tradition of the Eastern European Synagogue, Volume 2, Part 1, New York, Syracuse University Press, 2005, pp lxviii.

2. From Nofet Tzufim, by Pinchas ben Avraham Abba Shapira of Koretz (born 1728; died 10th of Elul, 1791), a disciple of the Ba' al Shem Tov and Maggid of Mezerich. (Published in Warsaw, 1929, pp 5-7). This teaching is reproduced in Louis I. Newman s Hasidic Anthology (New York: Schocken pbk, 1963), pp 456.

3. See, for example, Encyclopedia Judaica's article on "Bimah."

4. Thank you Eric Gold

5. My method usually involves memorizing what scale degree a song starts on and then the first few notes after that, i.e. "low 5, 1, 2, 3..." With a little bit of musical training, people can start to understand how to recognize scale degrees. And, of course, if you're trained enough to be able to write the melodies down, that's the best way of remembering it, as you'll have to process every single note. Ironically, when you're done writing the melody down, you know it well enough that you don't need to use what you just wrote.

6. IL Peretz, "A Gilgul Fun a Nign" ("The Metamorphosis of a Melody,") as reprinted and translated by Eli Katz: Katz, Eli. "IL Peretz; Selected Stories," 1991, New York, Zhitlowsky Foundation for Jewish Culture, pp 232.

7. Ibid. pp 236.

8. These ideas were inspired by similar concepts expressed by Mick Goodrick in "The Advancing Guitarist," 1987, Third Earth Productions, pp 98.

9. The term "Mode" usually includes an understanding of typical phrases in the musical style, making it more complex than a 'scale.'

10. In Ashkenazic Jewish music, that is. The topic of Arab-Jewish Maqam systems, is much too large a study for this work.

11. "Flat" means to "lower" the note, in these cases by one half step, or going one piano key to the left or one guitar fret to the left. If you see a "b" before a scale number, that means it's flatted.

12. The Greek scale that's related to it is called Phrygian. In Yiddish, we say "Freyg-ish" meaning, "like phrygian.

13. Every now and then you'll encounter melodies in 5, 7, 9 or other meters, but 3 and 4 will take you far enough.

14. Contrast this, to say a classical orchestra, in which there is unity and only unity - where at the down beat everyone's together, and in the middle of the measure. In Jewish music, there's more flexibility mid-measure, in terms of how the music is phrased.

15. Adapted from Buber, Martin. "Tales of the Chasidim." Schocken Books, New York, 1947 (1991 edition), pp 62-63.

16. Wohlberg, Max "The Music of the Synagogue" Jewish Music Council, (1947, revised 1963) pp 8.

17. Ibid. pp 9-10.

18. See Chapter 5 "Improvisations and variations on a melody..." and Chapter 6 "Jewish music theory."

19. See chapter 2 "Architecture..."

20. From the *Shabbat* Musaf Amidah

21. Smile, but consider keeping your body language more "contained" at the beginning, and "opening up" more as the class goes on, so that the class too, seems to "open up" over the hour. If you give all your energy in the opening round, you might not have it in you later when you really need it. Pace yourself!

22 See chapter 5 "How to sing a melody 20 times in a row"

23. Cutting off a talking session in a room of Jews is an art in its own right - remember to always be patient and respectful.

24. See Chapter 5: "How to sing a *nign* 20 times in a row" for more details.

25. I first learned this rhythmic teaching technique from multi-instrumentalist, Yiddish singer and educator Jeff Warschauer, who often uses dancing to teach people about rhythm and tempo.

26. See chapter 3

27. Such as the Metsudah Siddur, or Artscrolls "Interlinear Siddur" series.

28. See chapter 6 to learn about "minor" and "*freygish*."

29. Artscroll *siddur*im give very detailed instructions to the davener, which is very helpful for beginners.

30. That said, at very minimum you must be able to pronounce every word clearly and correctly, and really quite fluently, before you consider leading the congregation.

31. See chapter 1, "The Singing Core."

32. Faking it is not supposed to let you off the hook from properly learning the material - but only to say that realistically, mistakes will happen, especially at first, so don't compound them by alerting everybody every time you make a mistake.

33. Unless you're working in a tradition where the whole aesthetic is supposed to be 'everybody all the time', such as in certain Sephardic traditions.

34. Get to know your *amud* as a DRUMSET: Get there early, and search around to find a good 'bass' tone (usually there's one spot that really resonates low), and find a good place for a 'slap' or 'snare' sound, and create a simulated drumset on the amud.

35. See chapter 5, in the section called "Rhythm"

36. If you don't repeat words in your shul, then use nai-nai-nai's instead.

37. For those of you who understand musical notes, consider the following: many people can sing from around "A" below the treble staff up to around "D", which is a jump of almost an octave and a half. Because of that, the key of "D" is often a good starting place, as many melodies go as low as "Low 5," which would be that low A, and as high as "8" or "high D" or just a tad bit higher. Hence the key of D, which contains most of these notes, is a fairly safe bet Once again, the key of D isn't foolproof, so just do the best you can, with the majority of singers and that all-important 'atmosphere' we're after ever in mind. Remember, this isn't a perfect musical recording session: it's shul.

38. Shulchan Aruch, (Rabbi Yosef Karo 1560's), Part 1 Orach Chayim, ch 53, vs 11.

39. See chapter 2 "center of the room."

40. Of course, only get out of your seat when it won't be a distraction to what's already happening in the room.

41. *Seudah Shlishit* is one of my favorite times of *Shabbat*, where we sing slowly, so as not to rush out of *Shabbat*. Consider setting up in a small room with dimmed lights, and announce ahead of time that "this will be a time for singing and teaching, and we'll socialize later."

42. Quickly frame what you'll do - as in, very quickly - so that your introduction is only a small percentage of the length of the 'performance.' Even a quick 'shush' might do the trick - just so people know that something is about to happen.

GLOSSARY OF YIDDISH AND HEBREW TERMS

Amidah	Focal prayer of most Jewish services
amud	Table from which prayers are led and the torah is chanted
Ashkenazic	Jewish culture and tradition from Germany and Eastern Europe
ba'al tfilah (ba'a'lei tfilah)	Prayer leader(s)
Beit Hamikdash	Ancient holy Temple
bentsher	Book of blessings and songs used often on *Shabbat*
bimah	Raised platform in the synagogue from which prayers are led and torah chanted
bracha	Blessing
bulgar	Fast Jewish dance rhythm
chasidic	Lively Jewish traditions stemming from the famous Ba'al Shem Tov
chazzan (chazzonim)	Cantor (s)
chazzones	Cantorial music
chevre kadisha	Sacred burial society
daven	Pray
davener	One who is praying
dreys	Turns - in this case, ornaments around a melody
dveykus nign	Clinging *nign* - a melody that seeks union with the infinite
freygish	Scale found in Jewish music resembling Greek phrygian scale
freylakhs	Fast Jewish dance rhythm
gabbai (gabbaim)	Assistant(s) who make a prayer service function in various ways
Hakadosh Baruch Hu	The Holy Blessed One
half-Kaddish	Shorter version of a famous prayer that introduces many sections of the liturgy
havdallah	Ceremony marking the the end of *Shabbat*, and the beginning of the week
heimish	Homelike - intimate, close together, comfortable
hislav'vus nign	Burning *nign* - intense devotional melody
Kabbalat Shabbat	Service on Friday evening to welcome the *Shabbat*
kahal	Community
kapelye	Ensemble of klezmer musicians
kavanah	Sacred intentionality
kiddush	Blessing over the wine, and standing meal that follows in a shul
kishkes	Intestines, innards
klezmer	Musician, or music that was played by Eastern European Jews
Kohanim	The family that comes from the original high priests, the Cohens
Ladino	Spanish/Hebrew language spoken by some Sephardic Jews

Levites	Priests from the ancient holy temple
macher	Prominent person in the community who makes things happen
machol	Dance
makom	Special place
melave malka	Singing that takes place in the evening after *Shabbat*
menschlikhkeit	Being a decent human being
meshorer (meshoririm)	Chorister(s)
minhagim	Local traditions
minyan (minyanim)	Quorum of ten people required for certain communal prayers
musaf	Additional service following shacharit on *Shabbat* and holidays
nai nai nai	Meaningless syllables used to sing a *nign*
nign (nigunim)	Wordless melody
nusach	Chant of the cantor sung solo or with chordal accompaniment
Pirkei Avot	Ethics of the Fathers
piyut (piyutim)	Devotional poem-songs for special occasions in the Jewish year
rebbes	Rabbinic leaders of chassidic communities
Rebbetzin	Wife of a rebbe
rikud nign	Dance *nign*
Rosh Hashana	The holiday at the beginning of the Jewish year
Sephardic	Jewish cultures and traditions descended from Spanish Jewry
seudah shlishit	The third ceremonial meal eaten at the close of *Shabbat*
Sh'ma Yisroel	"Hear o' Israel..." the central proclamation of Jewish liturgy
Shabbat	The holy seventh day of the week (Hebrew)
Shabbos	The holy seventh day of the week (Yiddish)
shabbosdik	Appropriate for the holy day of *Shabbat*
shacharit	Morning services
shaliach (shlichei) tzibur	Prayer leader(s) of a community
shtibl	Small shul (usually chasidic)
shtender	Lectern from which prayers are led
shuckle (shuckling)	Rocking forwards and backwards during praying
shul	Synagogue
Shulchan Aruch	Central document of Jewish Law
siddur (siddurim)	Prayer book(s)
simcha	Joy, happiness - also a happy event
tisch	Table, a gathering at a table
tof	Drum
torah	The scroll of the five books of Moses
Y'varech'cha	Prayer blessing the Kohanim
Yiddish	German/Hebrew language of Eastern European Jews
Yism'chu	Rejoice on the *Shabbat*
zmirot	Special songs sung after meals on *Shabbat*

Joey Weisenberg is a mandolinist, guitarist, singer and percussionist based in New York City, who has performed and recorded internationally with dozens of bands in a wide variety of musical styles. Joey works as the Music Director at Brooklyn's oldest synagogue, the Kane Street Synagogue, and is the music faculty at Yeshivat Hadar, an egalitarian yeshiva in New York. He is an artist-fellow at the 14th Street Y's Laba program, and teaches klezmer music as a faculty member at KlezKanada. He was recently named to "36 under 36" in The Jewish Week as one of 36 new and exciting innovators in Jewish life today. Joey visits shuls and communities around the country as a musician-in-residence, in which he teaches his popular 'Spontaneous Jewish Choir' workshops.

For more information, please visit www.joeyweisenberg.com.

CPSIA information can be obtained
at www.ICGtesting.com
Printed in the USA
LVOW03s1335011117
554589LV00002B/170/P

9 780983 325307